the
JOY JOURNAL
for MAGICAL
everyday PLAY

the
JOY JOURNAL
for MAGICAL
everyday PLAY

Easy Activities & Creative Craft
for Kids and their Grown-ups

Written and illustrated by

LAURA BRAND

bluebird
books for life

First published in the United Kingdom 2020 by Bluebird,
an imprint of Pan Macmillan
The Smithson, 6 Briset Street, London EC1M 5NR
Associated companies throughout the world
www.panmacmillan.com

ISBN 978-1-5290-2559-0

1 3 5 7 9 8 6 4 2

A CIP catalogue record for this book is available from the British Library.

Typeset by Irissa Book Design
Printed and bound in Italy

Visit **www.panmacmillan.com** to read more about all our books
and to buy them. You will also find features, author interviews and
news of any author events, and you can sign up for e-newsletters
so that you're always first to hear about our new releases.

For My Husband & My Daughters...

Russell, thank you for always believing in me, encouraging me tenaciously and making sure I had everything I needed to write this book in a place of joy.

Mabel and Peggy, this is for you and because of you. Thank you for coming into this world the way you did and for making a mother of me. I love it.

X

Contents

'Parenting is a great adventure. Awakening your child's sense of curiosity and wonder helps you reawaken your own. Reawakening your own sense of curiosity and wonder helps you awaken your child's.'

Julia Cameron, *The Artist's Way for Parents*

Foreword

In this fast-paced modern world which is ruled by screens and punctuated with short concentration spans it can feel like an anxious time to be a parent. Most of us feel concerned about how much screen time our kids should or shouldn't have, how much plastic we're bringing into our homes with the temptation of the latest noisy and slightly annoying toy, and worry about if our children are spending enough time outside.

The modern world offers up little remedy to these concerns so the majority of us will find ourselves knee deep in plastic balls in the local soft play AGAIN or spending money on toys we wish we hadn't.

My long term darling friend Laura has come up with the most sensational bible of solutions to these tricky to navigate parental problems, which encourage us all to get back to basics.

Now let me tell you about Laura as I'm sure during this writing process she has been most modest and private when it comes to her own vivacity and glorious energy. We have been friends for over fifteen years and have been on many adventures together with some hilarious photos to prove it. I have always been magnetized to Laura's infectious need to try new things. She has worked every job imaginable – from bowling alley waitress to wardrobe organizer, with even a brief foray into pub singing (her rendition of *Sweet Child of Mine* is quite something) – and is never scared of the unknown. This latest venture is no different as she has gone with her gut and created something that is totally authentic and original. You can see on these pages that Laura has followed her intuition, her creativity flows perfectly thematically through the crafts and she has been bold with her ideas and the execution of them.

You'll no doubt fall in love with Laura's lust for life and aptitude for trying the new as you travel through this book. It's impossible not to.

I have a long term love of arts and crafts and adore nothing more than drawing and painting with my children, as I believe creativity is one of the most important outlets for us all. It doesn't have to be an immaculate masterpiece: it's simply the opportunity to dream, create and lose thought for a moment.

My dad was a sign writer throughout my childhood and has only just retired this year. I would sit in my dad's sign writing studio watching him hand paint ginormous, glossy letters effortlessly and all these years later the smell of paint fumes sends me rocketing back there. Art and design has been commonplace in my family for as long as I can remember. For me, drawing, making and creating has always been relaxing, cathartic and, as a child, a way to escape the confines of school and the academic curriculum I didn't feel I fitted into.

Being creative is something I'm passionate about keeping alive in the family now I have my own children. It's our 6 am go to when I can't take another episode of *Paw Patrol*. It's our rainy day must when we daren't go out into the downpour. It's our family happy space where we can create together regardless of age or ability.

Getting lost in creativity is not only a joy for our children but also for us shattered parents. When I'm in the flow of creativity, no matter how basic, I relax, breathe a little deeper and stop the constant mental rumination. This book is steeped in that notion and often in the most surprising of ways. I used to think I was being pretty inventive getting my kids to draw and paint on an old roll of wallpaper until my dear Laura and her fantastic book came along! Laura's ideas have led on to delightful tasks that bring to life ordinary ingredients and tools. Her imagination has transformed normal and often overlooked objects in our home and nature into fairy-tale fun. She has injected magic into the everyday things we forget about as we rush around with our faces in screens.

Vegetables, twigs, petals, flour: everyday things we don't usually associate with creativity have been given a new lease of life in this dreamy book.

Not only does this book emphasize how important creativity is but it also gets us to look at nature differently. It gets us mucky and grubby in the most glorious way. It encourages us to touch and squeeze and experience with all our senses.

I'm worried about how we are all dulling down the use of our senses these days as we spend so much less time really FEELING what is going on rather than just looking and judging and labelling. This book awakens our senses as we are encouraged to use our hands to experience creativity in a very visceral way.

Merging the most natural ingredients and tools with our own personal expression is very exciting all round.

If you're nervous about getting creative as you don't see yourself in that way, rest assured we are all capable of creativity and can use this book easily. It's not about creating perfection or even the intended outcome but instead it's about the whole process of trial and error, mess and commotion and the fun that comes with that.

It has taken me back to when I was a small girl in our back garden, with old glass bottles picking petals and dodging worms to make my own perfume. Mucky and grubby and so much fun in every way. We all need to allow our children to get messy and make mistakes especially in the modern world where we are often offered a vision of perfection we believe we have to live up to. We feel the pressure to be perfect parents, to have perfectly behaved children, to look perfect and be perfect, which is utter nonsense. We need to guide our children by example and allow them to delve into creation and the unknown. Otherwise we are left feeling an absence of joy and confidence. This book gives children the time and space to explore new themes, new sensations and ways of getting creative without the need to be perfect.

It's all about the process rather than the outcome.

I'm so thrilled Laura has created this special book and I can't wait to get stuck into it with my own children.

Fearne

Introduction

When I was pregnant with my first daughter, Mabel, I started a customized dungarees business from my kitchen table. It started off with a gift of brightly coloured and personalized painters' overalls for a best friend's birthday and as other friends started to enquire about them, turned into an enjoyable and busy enterprise in the last weeks of my pregnancy. I had no idea where this business would go, or for how long I would do it – it was a 'for now' project and it gave me so much joy. I decided to call my new business a Joy Journal Project, a work in progress, a changeable open format that I could alter along the way and something that would soon fit into my life as a joyful, new mum.

When I speak of joy, and I will mention it a lot through this book, I am referring to the smiley, warm flutter of contented bliss when you come into contact with something, someone or some place of peace and pleasure. Joy is a stronger emotion than happiness, it affects your brain, your circulatory and nervous systems. It also stimulates your production of dopamine and serotonin – the body's happy chemicals, which were flooding my body post-birth and certainly something that seems to come naturally to children.

Little did I realize as I rocked the baby bouncer with my feet, stitching name after name almost as rhythmically as the trusty BabyBjörn, that I was quietly reconnecting with and nourishing my own creative self. A part of me that had remained somewhat dormant after years of 'uncreative' jobs. I had forgotten what play and free flowing creativity felt like but I was reminded then that it was certainly good for my soul.

As a child I was always in the garden making mud pies, crushing petals into perfumes or making dens. A prominent memory from my childhood is the co-creation of an incredible 'hideaway' with my three best friends (who were siblings) after their grandparents donated their old garden shed to us. We painted it bright colours with wild flowers on the outside and old fabrics inside;

cushions, a table and chairs and most likely jars filled with murky, petal-perfumes. It was our pride and joy. We spent many summer days in our camp, receiving 'secret mail', as was instructed in writing above our letterbox – a small crack in the wood, just the right size for post – mostly received from their beloved grandparents who took on this task dutifully. When I think of the freedom we were granted to be creative and to play, I am so thankful because it is with that same permission that I wish to parent my own children.

The nostalgia, as I recount our beloved hideaway, reminds me of the person I was as a child and this is something I try to engage with during the activities I put together for my daughters, the ones you will find on the following pages in this book. Throughout each I strive to find a happy medium between gentle supervision, active participation and total presence.

Along with the experiences that I carefully chronicled and catalogued after the birth of my children, it took writing this book for me to realize that, through my creative play with them, my own joy had been reborn.

How to use this book

I decided to write this book because I wanted to bring together my homemade recipes, experiments and research of joyful things to do with my daughter, in a form that was easy to use at a moment's notice. A moment, being all you have in a lot of cases when entertaining young children!

When I was looking for games or craft ideas online, I would be put off by unusual ingredients or complicated instructions, but more than that I needed a little encouragement to let go, accept the mess of making and ENJOY the process too. I wanted to use the experience of play and craft as a time for bonding with my daughter instead of a quick distraction whilst I did something else. Of course I've included some fast, easy things to aid you at times when you can't give your full attention, but the main purpose of this book is to explore how to reignite creativity and a sense of play and share it with you.

In terms of ingredients, there is no reason why creative play with your children should cost the earth. The world around us is abundant in natural materials and I have kept this in mind where possible because I want this to work for everyone. I want you to feel confident in putting the activities in *The Joy Journal* into action and, beyond that, expand upon using your own environment, imagination and the tools you have available. I have included blank journal pages after each chapter for you to note down your observations along the way as well as for brainstorming ideas that personalize the recipes and activities, whether that's amending measurements or adding your own creative magic, which I hugely encourage.

Each activity is broken down into the key areas of interest for any parent or carer. For each one I asked myself these questions: What do we need? What is the potential for mess? How long will we be doing this until boredom strikes? Will I (the adult) be into it? What is this activity teaching us?

This creative manual of fifty or so crafty ideas and activities is written completely honestly – with all the ups and downs, tantrums (both mother and daughter!) and rejected attempts at fun, we have had along the way.

When I started writing this book, Mabel my eldest was just two while Peggy was five months old, and now they are sixteen months and approaching three years, it's been quite a journey of discovery. I have gone from exploring play that works for a toddler whilst having a babe in arms to learning about harmonious joint activities and parallel play, as between them they work out which one of them is boss!

There is pure joy to be had in a shared experience and in the golden moments of connection with your child, when you realize you are totally in the present enjoying the freedom to play and connect with not only your little ones, but with your essential self.

Tool box of joy

To make play with your children easy and stress-free, I have created a tool box which includes everything you will need for the activities in this book. You can find many of the items around the home already and I have divided the tool box up into kitchen, bathroom, pantry, craft, and bits and bobs to make it easier to locate everything!

A few of the activities in this book are definitely enhanced by a little imagination, and sometimes I might suggest you use items from nature or further bits and bobs, which I have included under the heading 'Inspire Me' . . .

KITCHEN CUPBOARDS

Baking parchment

Baking tray

Cheese grater

Cookie cutters
(variety of shapes/sizes)

Cupcake cases

Cupcake tray

Cups and saucers

Empty cereal boxes

Flour/sugar shaker

Fork

Heatproof/freezer-friendly bowl

Ice cube tray

Jam jars (with lids)

Measuring cups/scales

Measuring jug

Mixing bowls (variety of sizes)

Pans (variety of sizes)

Paper straws

Plates

Rolling pin

Scrubbing brush

Sieve

Small bowls

Spatula

Tablespoon

Teaspoon

Tea towels

Tongs

Tray

Washing-up liquid

Whisk

PANTRY

Cooking oil

Cornflour

Food colouring

Fruit and veg (e.g. apples, oranges, red peppers, celery, strawberries)

Honey/agave syrup

Lemons

Oats (rolled and ground)

Plain flour

Powdered vegetable (for colouring, e.g. beetroot, spinach)

Rice (uncooked)

Seeds/nuts

Table salt

BATHROOM

Epsom salts

Liquid body soap

Nail brush

Old toothbrush

Sensitive skin shaving foam

Soap bar

Sponge

CRAFT CUPBOARD

Air dry clay

Coloured pencils

Crayons

Felt-tip pens

Kraft paper roll

Lollipop sticks

Paint (acrylic, watercolour, poster or ready-mixed paint)

Paintbrushes

Paper (plain, coloured, patterned)

Pen

Pritt stick

PVA glue

Scissors

Sellotape

Stickers

Tissue paper

Twine/string

White crayon

Wool

BITS AND BOBS

Basket

Cloth

Compost

Document folder/A4 envelope

Flower seeds

Torch

A NOTE ON MEASUREMENTS

I use cups to measure out everything – for me, this just makes life that bit easier and setting up activities quicker. However, if you don't have measuring cups, here is a very quick conversation chart.

FOR DRY INGREDIENTS

1 cup = 136g

½ cup = 68g

¼ cup = 34g

FOR WET INGREDIENTS

1 cup = 236ml

½ cup = 118ml

¼ cup = 59ml

Inspire me

This page is meant to be a starting point for you until you find your flow. I have often had to refer to Pinterest or Instagram to spark my creativity and give an activity a good push off.

I will sometimes refer to 'loose parts', which is basically a collection of materials that are used in play with no given direction, so they allow the child to explore on their own, with curiosity and imagination. Loose parts could be natural (sticks, rocks, shells, feathers, pine cones, tree bark, flowers) or man-made (yogurt pots, wooden pegs, nuts and bolts, pom-poms, bowls, spoons, funnels, buttons) – the possibilities are endless. Having loose parts available to play with will stimulate your child's creativity, and they are readily available in some form most of the time, which makes life easy for us, the parents!

A few of our favourites are:

IN NATURE

Acorns
Bark
Dried flowers
Feathers
Fresh flowers
Grass
Leaves
Moss
Pebbles

Petals
Pine cones
Sand
Shells
Soil
Sticks

BITS AND BOBS

Buttons
Corts
Cutlery
Dried beans
Dried pasta
Egg cartons
Fabric scraps

Kitchen roll
Kitchen/toilet roll tubes
Paper scraps
Pipe cleaners
Pom-poms
Ribbons
Wooden pegs

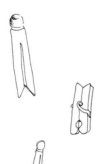

*Please note that this list for loose-part play should be adapted according to the age of your child, to avoid any items that may cause choking – see Creating a Safe Space (see page 29), for more on this.

The good stuff

Sure enough, my daughters Mabel and Peggy seem to reach 'milestones' at different times, they like different foods and they handle social situations like chalk and cheese. Celebrating 'uniqueness' is very important to me, and although I do enjoy reading about and understanding the developmental stages of a child, obsessing over them is unhelpful and unnecessary and will affect the creative flow that we are setting out to find within the joyful crafts and play activities in this book.

However, just in case it's not easy for you to get invested immediately in frivolous and free play (certainly not the messy sort), with the developmental stages in mind I have created a simplified list of really 'good stuff' that I reckon we all want to know our children are benefiting from and experiencing while they play. Certainly, I know that if I can tick any of these boxes during time spent away from my phone and engaged with my daughters, I get a surge of feel-good factor.

In each section you will see these things are referred to in specific activities, so you can feel safe in the knowledge that the fun you are both having is also holistically important.

Adventure	Creativity	Nurture
Body work	Emotion	Self-care
Bonding	Imagination	Senses
Care for animals	Listening	Speaking
Confidence	Nature	Thinking

Things to remember

It is really hard to try new things, let alone under the pressure of a bored child, which is why I want to share my checklist of things that I do in order to mentally reboot when I feel like I'm being beaten by the intensity of parenthood.

STAY PRESENT IN THE PROCESS

Being available throughout the process of play and creativity and not being focused entirely on an end result will ensure a much more rounded, happy and calm experience. If you see your child enjoying a walk, distracted by everything along their path – a beetle, a blade of grass, a crack in the pavement – then perhaps you can allow that curiosity to take you both on its own journey, rather than imagining that the joy can only be found at a certain destination.

EMBRACE THE MESS

I know this statement will seem crazy, as mess is, after all, something we are conditioned to think is bad and unhealthy and not very Marie Kondo (who I love, by the way). I just mean, if things can be wiped, cleaned or cleared away, then don't lose your peace of mind over it. In this moment, know that imperfection is okay, because sometimes there is magic to be found in the mess . . .

BE MINDFUL AS YOU GO

Being aware of how you are feeling moment to moment and being present to see if your child's mood changes will help you to accept every situation as it is. Young children are not always able to express their own varying emotions plainly, but you may be able to read the signs and then be able to shift gear if there is a need for action.

SEEK JOY

This is about opening our eyes to the world around us and looking out for the things that make us smile spontaneously or give us delight in that moment. I sometimes ask myself, when challenged, can I find joy in this moment? If I stop and take a second to acknowledge my surroundings, I nearly always find there is something positive to connect with that is beyond myself.

POSITIVE REDIRECTION

This is important, and it's something that I struggle with most days. With two small children at my feet there is toddler frustration, sibling rivalry and my own potential for impatience. Positive redirecting, simply put, is 'showing them what to do' rather

than 'what not to do', and offering an alternative activity if the current one is not inspiring them. I have written 'Positive redirection!' on a Post-it note that's stuck on the fridge, just to remind me!

CHANGE THE ENVIRONMENT

Taking yourself and your child into a different setting – be that away from a group or outside into fresh air – can often decompress a situation that is starting to get a little out of control. The change in surroundings will offer different sensations, as well as provide space for calm and quiet sanctuary.

TRUST PLAY

It is not always a natural inclination for adults to 'play', and by play I mean engaging in an open-ended activity for pure enjoyment, with no purpose. Dr Stuart Brown, who started The National Institute for Play in California, has done wonderful interviews and a brilliant Ted Talk on the benefits of play for adults and children. In these he reiterates time and time again that 'Play, including physical activity or sports, a creative practice like painting or simply giggling with your child, will improve your physical and emotional well-being'. He also states that 'Play is the purest expression of love'. Surely this is the sort of encouragement we need to let down our hair and to nourish ourselves and our children?

ENCOURAGE AND PRAISE

When it comes to encouragement and praise for my daughters and whatever creation may be in front of us, it's important to me that it's balanced enough that they don't feel they have to reach a certain level of achievement before gaining my attention. It is a Montessori approach that I find most helpful in this area (elaborated

on with expertise in the book *The Montessori Toddler* by Simone Davies) and that is to give feedback on what they have done using positive descriptions rather than it being about the end goal. Because we focus so much on the process in the following activities – these will be a good opportunities for you to give positive encouragement and describe what you can see happening, rather than the finished article. I believe this also helps build their confidence in thinking outside of the box and allowing space for joyful creativity.

PUT THE PHONE DOWN

When I'm looking at my phone, I am not present. When I am not present, accidents happen and tempers start to flare. Putting my phone aside is always a good idea, but it usually takes a nudge to remind me to do so.

REMEMBER, YOU ARE DOING A GREAT JOB

This is a simple affirmation that we ALL need to tell ourselves at times.

ENJOY WHERE YOU ARE

Appreciate your surroundings, look at your children engaging with whatever it is they are doing right now, and just for a moment be grateful for this time.

Creating a safe space

I have tried and tested each of the activities in this book with my own two-year-old (and my one-year-old usually at our side), making amendments for ease and, for the most part, keeping things completely toddler friendly. To ensure that I have covered all areas, and for your peace of mind, I have included here a preparatory guide not only to give yourself the best chance of fully immersed play, but to ensure that your kids stay safe in the process, too.

WATER PLAY

Most importantly, always supervise water play, be that during bathtime or during sensory play activities that use other vessels. Check the water temperature before letting your kids dive in, ensuring that it isn't too hot when they put their hands in, in recipes like homemade Play Dough (see page 45). Use fresh water for all water play, for good hygiene.

To prevent any slips and falls, dry any wet floor areas as you go, or, even better, place a bath mat or towel on the floor when preparing your play space.

SMALL PARTS

Close supervision is required for any small-part play, and when in doubt, I recommend exclusion of small items for children under the age of three years old.

TOOLS

Don't leave sharp tools like scissors or knives near your children. Keep them well out of reach during the activities, and in some cases it may be beneficial to prepare any cutting ahead of time – this preserves sanity, too!

Use of ribbons, string and any long items that could get tangled should also be supervised for children under the age of three.

ALLERGIES

Some activities include food items or soap products. I use organic, baby-sensitive and child-friendly ingredients in all the recipes you will find in this book; however, please do not use anything that you think your child might be allergic to (e.g. nuts). If your

child has any known skin conditions or if you have any doubts, please seek professional advice. If you are doing activities with other people's children (see playdates on page 186), check with their parents for any allergies.

STORAGE

Certain activities require that leftovers or homemade materials are stored for further use. I recommend that all homemade products in this book have a one-week shelf life and should be stored in a cool, dry place out of sunlight and in a clearly labelled container.

SUPERVISION

I have collated activities suitable for children of two years upwards; however, I advise that you yourself decide on the appropriate activities for your own child based on their personal development and interest in them. All activities in this book should be participated in (for the pure joy of it) or at the very least supervised by an adult.

Being kind to the planet

With an ever-increasing awareness for the well-being of our planet, we have the opportunity to bring up our children to be conscious of their imprint on the world around us. This isn't a book about creating a zero-waste home, but if we can play our part, however great or small, it will make a difference.

RECYCLE

Check with your local council as to how to organize your recycling (everywhere is different). Keep in mind to minimize single-use plastics in your craft activities and include your kids in the process of recycling. Clearly label the bins to make it easy for everyone to clear away.

REPURPOSE

Can it be used again? So many items can be, especially for arts and crafts and creative play.

Bottles filled with rice or lentils make wonderful instruments. The cardboard innards of toilet and kitchen rolls can become both megaphones and telescopes. Cereal boxes can be re-used for drawing on, or for making templates (see pages 162-3) or shadow puppets (see page 150), while old clothes, if not being given to charity, can be used as painting overalls or for dressing-up clothes. These materials can also be cut up into cloths – something else that will come in handy during these activities!

RESPECT

With a lot of activities aimed at getting our kids out into nature, it's important to remind them to be kind in nature, too – to insects, animals and living growing plants. In our household we say, 'BE CURIOUS and KIND'. Encouraging our children to explore nature is important, for example looking under logs or following snail's trails, but we should never forget that these flora and fauna are living their lives, too and tread carefully.

'The second reason creativity is so fascinating is that when we are involved in it, we feel that we are living more fully than during the rest of life.'

Mihaly Csikszentmihalyi,
Creativity: Flow and the Psychology
of Discovery and Invention

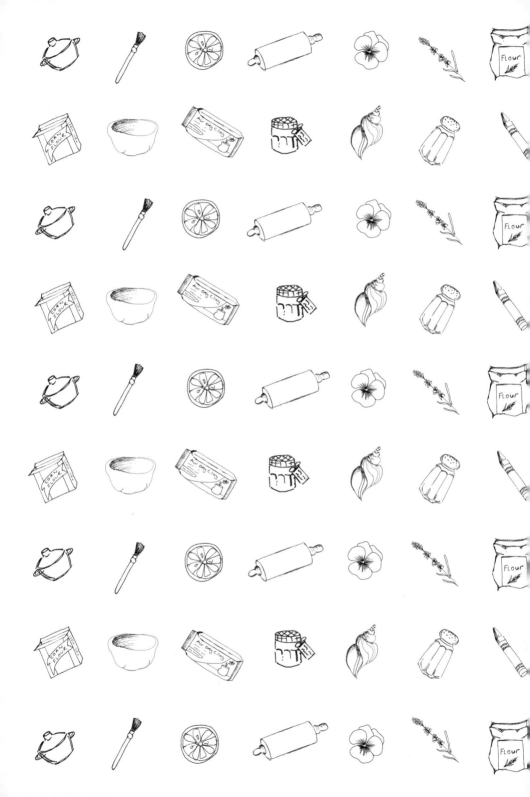

Rainy Days

With all the good will in the world, I find it hard when it rains (and when it doesn't) not to be drawn into the world of Netflix and the never-ending episodes of Hey Duggee! *as an entertainment tool for my children when I'm busy. The only conflict comes when the countdown to the next episode doesn't start quite soon enough for my daughter, so I scramble around for the remote exclaiming, 'YES! I DO WANT TO WATCH THE NEXT EPISODE! Need you ask?'*

Before we had children we said definitely NO screen time – how naive of us to think it would be so easy? Of course, that went out of the window as soon as the post-birth hormones wore off, I was absolutely exhausted and at an all-time low in terms of self-care. I remember the first time I put on a YouTube video of nursery rhymes – Mabel was maybe seven months old – and it was a breakthrough . . . Mabel was in the next room, quietly captivated by a song about a snowflake – it wasn't even Christmas. I think I took a shower. A shower in a bathroom, on my own! I know I felt guilty about this at the time; I knew on some level what I was letting myself into. It seems much less of a big deal the second time, the third time, the fourth time . . .

As she got older and, in this case, when I was newly pregnant and caring for my 12-month-old from the bathroom floor, bent double with Hyperemesis, there was nothing more soothing in the world than Makka Pakka washing his stones. I was so unwell that I caved in at every opportunity. With every gut-wrenching chuck, I was hitting that play button faster than I could say 'two under two'.

For convenience purposes, we invested in a small device that can be used in the car, on a plane, or in her bedroom (propped up against a Beatrix Potter ornament at just the right angle to be seen from the cot). It is a solution, we feel, for any occasion and although I am not pregnant and struggling while writing this, it has been a wintery, rainy week and I am still thankful for some screen time, but not dependent on it.

This is the perfect time to get creative, imaginative and hunker down with a craft box, so I am going to break down a few simple, stress-free, rainy day activities. I will set them out for you in a digestible form so you know exactly what's in store and you can embark on these crafts with joy instead of horror.

So ... let's chase away that rainy day boredom.

Pinch pots (and other stories)

WHAT YOU WILL NEED

Air dry clay

Baking parchment

Rolling pin (if making hand prints only)

Cookie cutter (if making hand prints only)

Loose parts

Small bowl of water

Water and PVA glue ratio 1:1, or Homemade Glaze (see page 61), for sealing before painting

POTENTIAL FOR MESS

Air dry clay has a tendency to stick to hands, so have a bowl of soapy water and a towel at the ready for afterwards!

ENGAGED FOR

About 30 minutes (but remember you can return to this activity in a few days' time to admire, paint or glaze your pots).

PARENTAL ENJOYMENT

This is one of the most satisfying activities in the book for grown-ups, and is something I personally do without my daughter sometimes, because of the mindful effect it has on me. I always feel deeply engaged with the process of handling clay and the results are always pleasing.

GOOD STUFF

Bonding

Confidence

Creativity

Imagination

Listening

Nature

Senses

METHOD

Using air dry clay is probably my favourite craft memory from childhood. I distinctly remember a massive block of Early Learning Centre clay that I dipped in and out of for what seemed like months on end (how was it not drying out!?), making never-ending trinket plates, hand-painted and scribed into with 'Made by Laura '97' and a love heart and a kiss, always. I have happily noticed a resurgence of clay work in the last few years among the adult craft community, and I follow many an Instagram page of cool studios and pottery cafés, always hopeful of convincing friends to come and join me, perhaps in making some oddly shaped tableware.

It makes sense that clay is a popular medium, because right from the mindful moments of shaping and rolling it in your hands through to seeing the finished product (that has the potential for being used to present food, as a gift to a grandparent or simply for storing bits and bobs), it is truly satisfying and calming, unless you are wrangling a toddler at the end of a very long day, to hurriedly make a Father's Day gift . . . This was us; we sat for a moment, Mabel and I, before she took the ball of clay in her hand and lobbed it at the wall. I promptly admitted defeat at the once sweetly imagined idea of a bonding/making session, and after she went to bed, I continued on my own and had a glorious time trying things out, better preparing myself for the next attempt . . .

So, after that experience, I decided that anything requiring Mabel to sit and listen to an instruction should be done in the morning, and I chose a fresh faced 10am slot a couple of days later to try again, when we were both full of creative spirit. Peggy was awake, too, playing with some toys, and so with both girls present and happy, I decided we would start with a beginners' clay experience that could double up as the present for their dad that we hadn't got round to sorting previously.

HAND PRINTS

We rolled out small balls of clay on a piece of baking parchment with a rolling pin, then, once they were flat but not too thin, we got little Peggy's hand and pressed it into the clay so it moulded slightly around her fingers and created an adorable squidgy handprint. Mabel loved to help with this, and it really engaged her – she understood the fragility of the clay as it took a couple of attempts to stop Peggy from scratching her nails into it, making the print unrecognizable! Once we got a successful hand shape, we set Peggy's aside and we went on to do Mabel's, who preferred the idea of drawing around her hand with a pencil. With both these little girls' handprints now presented, in their own unique styles, we cut round them using a cookie cutter to shape them into discs and then to finish I used ten-year-old Laura's method of scratching some wording onto the discs around the handprints and added the date for that extra layer of nostalgia.

We had 24 hours to get these ready for Father's Day, so we had to cheat the process a bit, as we were in a hurry and didn't have the time to let them dry naturally. I put them onto a baking tray in a cold oven and popped the temperature to 150°C/130°C Fan/300°F, checking on them every 15 minutes until they had totally dried. These took about 45 minutes but it will depend on the size of your project. A note: the reason you put them into a cold oven is to prevent them hitting the heat right away and cracking.

These special gifts were a total hit and with our new-found clay confidence and skills, we subsequently set about a family craft session, Dad included, making Pinch Pots.

PINCH POTS

Take a fist-size piece of the clay and roll it into a ball using your palms – don't get your fingers involved as it will prevent the ball getting a smooth, even finish, so when you are rolling, instruct the family to roll 'palm to palm'. This part is surprisingly relaxing, so enjoy the feeling of the clay shaping and heating in your palms. Once the clay feels like a perfectly round ball (or as close to that as you can), you can put it onto

1

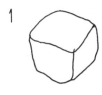

2

3

the table in front of you and press your thumb boldly into the very centre, firmly and confidently. You want to push down as far as you can without being able to feel the table through the bottom. You may need to help your little one get started with this, so unlike 'put your own lifejacket on first', help them before you do your own, otherwise frustration might kick in!

Then, I think it's easiest then to pick up the clay in your non-pinching hand and pinch your way around the edges with your strongest pointing finger and thumb, turning as you go. This part can continue until you feel that the pot is nicely formed. Pinch it out any way you want it.

Mabel and I had prepared for this activity with some natural finds from the garden to stamp onto the clay, and we played around by printing leaves (vein side down) and succulents, with their gorgeous rose-like definition, into the centre of our little pots. (Have a look at the natural loose parts suggestions on page 22 and decide what thing you think might make beautiful patterns in the clay.) We carefully put our pots onto baking paper on a tray and left them in the sunlight to dry – ours took three days in a dry environment – but if you're in a hurry you can use the oven method on page 40.

Air dry clay can be painted using acrylic paint, and to seal your pinch pots and clay decorations you can use Homemade Glaze (see page 61) or a mix of equal parts water and PVA glue. While either solution can be painted on to seal and protect your pieces, air dry clay cannot hold liquids, so, sadly, no coffee cups!

Indoor treasure hunt

WHAT YOU WILL NEED

Clues – we used easy peel stickers

Piece of paper

Pen

Fancy dress (optional)

Treasure

ENGAGED FOR

Around 30–45 minutes.

PARENTAL ENJOYMENT

This game reminds me what it is like to play in adulthood. Wear hats and get into character!

GOOD STUFF

Adventure

Body work

Bonding

Confidence

Imagination

Thinking

POTENTIAL FOR MESS

Depends on what you are using as clues and treasure – we used stickers that peel off easily, which meant zero tidying up because we collected them as we went.

METHOD

What do you do on a rainy weekend morning when you are unmotivated to leave the house? On this particularly bleak Saturday, we were all home as a family and boredom had struck, early doors. My husband suggested an indoor treasure hunt. I didn't think we had the right gear. What about the clues? What about the prize? What about the energy? I thought, as I stared into my coffee.

There is no denying that I needed a bit of encouragement to get into the spirit of a treasure hunt. I was tired, uninspired and the thought of chasing around and looking for things, pretending I didn't know where the clues were leading us, felt a stretch too far. That's the thing with parenthood, though; I totally believe in self-care but Saturday morning family time is no place for a take-it-easy attitude. No parent is rolling back into bed at 9am on a weekend to watch movies, eat take-away food and sleep until they can sleep no more . . . are they?!

At this moment, husband and daughter march into the kitchen wearing a policeman's hat, a pirate's hat and brandishing a sort of Crocodile Dundee number for me, shouting in unison, 'Come on, Mummy! Let's play!' How could I refuse? I was put in charge of drawing out the clues; for this we used a sheet of easy peel stickers that were in the art cupboard. I replicated as best I could, on a sheet of A4, pictures of the chosen stickers with a little tick box by each. The stickers themselves were then thoughtfully put around the house by PC Husband (the policeman's hat was a child's size: tacky, plastic and perched adorably on the top of his head – just for the mental image) and with both parents now fully invested creatively, it got a little more serious. A sense of urgency suddenly descended on the treasure hunters, Mabel completely captivated as she held her clue sheet, and we started the search with dedication.

As yet, the treasure hadn't even been decided on, and the reason I am telling you this is that I want to get the point across that improvization, spontaneity and being in the moment are key components of successful play. Everything was unfolding as it was, with no prep or planning, and there was no need for a big prize at the end, because we were allowing it to happen organically, enjoying the process as much as our daughter was. We trusted that we would think of something 'high stake', something we already had in the house, by the time we came to the final stretch, but the imperfection of this was in itself quite liberating.

We were now hunting for the stickers, ticking off each as we went … I had done myself proud on the drawing front, as thankfully everything was easily recognizable on the clue sheet. We were halfway through and I finally decided on the treasure and hid it by the final sticker. I should also mention that as each sticker was located it was unpeeled and stuck onto our clue sheet – that's important to note

because … no tidying up afterwards, it's being sorted as you go!

Sometimes we were soldiers crawling on the floor, sometimes rolling from one clue to another – whatever we could think of to make the experience immersive and different, with no prep or tools. The dressing-up items made a difference, too; it was simple but it took us out of ourselves. We looked silly and it didn't matter – it was the not-caring that was so much fun.

Last clue on the page was a rabbit picture … and our adventure had brought us to Mabel's bedroom. Stuck onto her cot was the rabbit sticker next to her treasure. She was happy. She felt she'd achieved a great thing in finding the treasure, her favourite food, a Babybel in all of its red, shiny goodness, clutched in the paws of her favourite night-time cuddly bunny. And so did we, we'd achieved quality family time at home, filled with laughter and joy.

Play dough

WHAT YOU WILL NEED

2 small bowls

Large mixing bowl

Wooden spoon

1/2 cup plain flour

1/4 cup table salt

1/4 cup warm water

1 tsp cooking oil

Half a lemon

OPTIONAL

Colouring – if using liquid colour (i.e. food colouring) add 2–4 tsp to the water. For powdered colour (i.e. powdered vegetable such as beetroot or spinach) add 2 tsp to the flour

Loose parts

POTENTIAL FOR MESS

Fairly high. A toddler and a bowl of flour will mean a light dusting over all the surrounding surfaces. Also, be mindful that (age dependent) they may try to eat the dough. I have a trick to help reduce some of the mess, but I cannot guarantee a spotless exercise.

ENGAGED FOR

Roughly 45 minutes– 1 hour. They will still be playing with it for days afterwards.

PARENTAL ENJOYMENT

High. Good news . . . it is proven that creative hand use is stress-relieving and anxiety lessening. Kneading dough is therefore good for our mental health! Add lavender for an extra 'ahhhh' factor.

GOOD STUFF

Bonding

Creativity

Imagination

Listening

Senses

Thinking

METHOD

Play dough is the gift that keeps on giving. There is a reason why the famous brand has existed since the mid-1950s, selling millions of pots a year, with its comforting, familiar smell and endless opportunities for play and craft. Homemade play dough is our favourite activity in this book, because it is so simple and it is the perfect communal or independent activity. If I have the time and inclination, I will make play dough after the kids have gone to bed, ready for the next morning, but I have also found a way of doing this with Mabel that works in a harmonious way.

I measure out the flour, salt and oil myself and put everything into small bowls, set out on a tray or a toddler-height table, with a big mixing bowl, a cup of warm water and a wooden spoon. Allow your 'creative partner' to mix the dry ingredients together in the bowl until flour, salt and dry

colouring (if using)are completely combined. Ask them to squeeze the half lemon into the bowl (pick out any pips!) and continue to stir. If using liquid colouring, add it now – try food colouring, watercolour paint or vegetable dye. Remember: dry colouring should be added to the dry ingredients or liquid colouring (food colouring) to the water before mixing otherwise it won't combine properly.

Now for the messy bit! The warm water needs to be slowly poured onto the mixture, just a little at a time while stirring until it is combined enough to throw caution to the wind and let them start using their eager hands! In no time at all it will become a doughy, crumbly mass that can be tipped onto a clean dry surface, ready to be kneaded.

Just to make sense of the whole process and why we use these particular ingredients, I'll break it

down. The flour and water combine to make the base: warm water reacts with the proteins in the flour and makes it stretchy. The salt acts as a preservative, the lemon adds elasticity and the oil produces the smooth, non-sticky texture.

If it is too dry, add a spoonful of water; if it is too wet, add a spoonful of flour then keep on kneading – you want to create a dough that doesn't stick to the hands but holds its shape well. We usually make a little batch each so we can do this at the same time, allowing each of us to choose our own colour to add to our water (this is a good practice session for a playdate, too).

The beauty of this activity is that when we do this together I feel like we are in total harmony with one another. There is a meditative quality to kneading dough, which is clearly effective for even the liveliest of toddlers or stressed-out parents!

ADDING IN LOOSE PART PLAY

The idea of adding loose parts to the play is to push the imagination and creativity a little further and get everyone thinking outside the box. I have listed some ideas for loose parts in the Inspire Me section (see page 22). To get into the flow of loose part play, why don't you start off with play dough cupcakes using paper cases, or cut out cookie shapes and add sprinklings of dried and freshly picked flowers or herbs?

TIP

Play dough will be good for about a week if stored in a sealed, air tight container in a cool place. However, as with anything made using kitchen ingredients, if it starts to look weird or smell . . . chuck it out and start again!

Moon sand

WHAT YOU WILL NEED

2 cups plain flour

Large mixing bowl

60ml cooking oil

Tray

Cups/cookie cutters (optional)

POTENTIAL FOR MESS

I would be lying if I said this was mess-free. My husband took one look at our daughter playing with moon sand and opted out of this one!

ENGAGED FOR

5 minutes to make, 25–45 minutes of messy play.

PARENTAL ENJOYMENT

This depends on the parent! If you are someone who does NOT like sand (i.e. 'I am a pool person, not a beach person'), this probably isn't the activity for you.

GOOD STUFF

Creativity

Listening

Senses

Imagination

METHOD

Before settling on this 'kitchen pantry' recipe I had twice tried to make mouldable sand with my daughter, using actual sand. However, I couldn't succeed (and so it is still a work in progress); it was either too solid or too sludgy and I didn't find sand itself that easy to acquire in a small quantity. I am sure my husband (who hates sand) will think of this quite differently, but I felt we'd really made a fantastic breakthrough when I discovered that flour can be mixed with oil to create the perfect consistency.

Put the flour into a large mixing bowl, pour in the oil and get your toddler mixing it with their hands (think 'apple crumble topping'), rubbing it between fingertips up high, so it falls back into the bowl and forms sandy coloured thin breadcrumbs.

Keep going until it's almost like sand, then, if you are ready for it, tip it out onto a tray. Add fun things at this point like little cups to fill and tip upside down like sandcastles, or shaped cookie cutters – you can use your imagination here to see what tools are around your kitchen. This has the potential to be a fantastically focused activity; it was incredibly fun for Mabel, and I was thrilled that flour and oil had created a magical assortment of sandy shapes.

However, the excitement the first time we tried this did go a little OTT and Mabel must have confused my instruction of 'mix the sand like it is crumble' with 'eat this utterly delicious apple crumble', because great handfuls of the stuff were being consumed at an almighty rate – which is when sand-phobic Dad walked in and declared this a horrible activity and winced at the idea that she might be chewing on actual grains of stone from the southern coastline.

Once cleared up (and all it actually took was to scrape it back from the cups and cookie cutters into the tray, turning a blind eye to the ingested bits), the moon sand was requested several times that week. It will keep for about a week in a sealed, air tight container. We made it again – no eating this time – and I gave Mabel little sea life toys to incorporate into this sensory play, which extended the imaginative quality of the activity hugely. It has become our go-to quiet time tray of joy.

Kitchen rock band

WHAT YOU WILL NEED

Pots/pans/other containers that can be bashed!

2 wooden spoons

Spatula

Whisk

Ear plugs (optional)

ENGAGED FOR

How long can you stand the sound?! I think my kids would make noise day and night if they could – they basically do, but realistically . . .

the kitchen rock band has its limits: just let them punch themselves out a bit before ending their gig!

POTENTIAL FOR MESS

Get the kids to help put the pots and pans away afterwards and then it is a zero mess activity!

PARENTAL ENJOYMENT

I enjoy a good bang on a saucepan with a wooden spoon, who doesn't? It's cathartic for all ages.

GOOD STUFF

Body work

Bonding

Confidence

Emotion

Imagination

Speaking

METHOD

If your child likes to make a noise, this one is for you! Think about using different containers and utensils and giving your child free rein to do something that seems a bit 'out of the box' – just give them the tools and let them bash out some tunes!

This is a really positive way to channel excess energy, and if you want to participate too, you might just find your inner rock star is thankful for it.

Painted scenes and backdrops for play

SHORT
&
SWEET

WHAT YOU WILL NEED

Paper

Paint

Toys appropriate for your backdrop

METHOD

For those days that require a little nudge of inspiration, we create painted backdrops and scenes to accompany our play. When using the small sea and water toy creatures, we might make a finger-painted sea bed, waves and dots of sand. Perhaps we need to paint a red-and-white checked blanket with little cups of tea or snacks on, for an urgent teddy bears' picnic...

Remember, you will have to let these works of art dry, so have some fun designing and painting your scene on the paper then leave to dry overnight ready for the next day. Keep them safe and bring them out time and time again.

Colour hunting

WHAT YOU WILL NEED

Coloured pens, pencils or crayons

Paper

Tray

ENGAGED FOR

20–45 minutes, make it last however long you want!

POTENTIAL FOR MESS

No mess

PARENTAL ENJOYMENT

This is actually so quick and easy and satisfying. It really helps our children to recognize colours and objects, and exercises their use of language, thinking as well as getting everyone moving. It ticks a lot of boxes.

GOOD STUFF

Adventure

Body work

Bonding

Confidence

Listening

Speaking

Thinking

METHOD

A fast, energy-busting, indoor or outdoor activity that engages your child in play whilst also helping them with colour recognition.

Get a piece of paper and put it onto a tray. Using 4 to 6 different coloured crayons/pens or pencils draw a box in each colour. Now send your child off around the house or go with them around the garden or park and find as many items as you can in those colours, filling the tray.

An invitation to play

In the Inspire Me section of this book (see page 22), I have written about 'loose parts', introducing you to the idea of items that can be used for open-ended play and props. An invitation to play encourages your kids to play in an imaginative, creative and interesting way in a space facilitated by us, the grown-ups. It's very simple, yet very effective, and it is a great activity for rainy days, for siblings to do together, or for playdates as well as solo play.

To create an invitation to play, set out a few items (loose parts) or toys, in an appealing way. I like to use small bowls, baskets and trays to present items clearly. With this activity, we are just giving the children the starting point, then allowing them to lead and express themselves, so although you may have set this up with precision, thought and a clear outcome in mind, this will be practice in letting go and finding the joy in observing what happens naturally, when your children are given permission to express themselves and direct their own play.

Here are some ideas for invitations to play, that we have had fun with at home . . .

AT THE TABLE

Small teacups and saucers

Small jug of water

Tea towel cut into small squares to make mini dish cloths

Teaspoons

A small bowl of dried lavender heads and rosebuds

MOON SAND TRAY

A batch of moon sand (see page 48) in a tray

An empty tray or baking tray

Small stacking cups

A fork

Small figurines – animals, insects, sea creatures

PLAY DOUGH FOSSILS

A batch of play dough (see page 45)

Shells

Tongs

Magnifying glass

A small bowl of soil

A paintbrush

It is a good idea to think about what your child might do with the items, as this will help you set up the space, but remember – leave room for the unexpected!

Homemade finger paint

WHAT YOU WILL NEED

1 tbsp flour
1 tsp cornflour
Mixing bowl
Food colouring
50ml warm water
Spoon
Plate

METHOD

A friend posted on Facebook asking if anyone knew of any non-toxic, inexpensive craft paint to buy, as she was unhappy about the amount of ingredients going into shop-bought paint. It inspired me to have a go at making a batch of homemade messy paint. This recipe is gloopy enough for finger painting, great for handprints and dries within 10 minutes.

Mix the dry ingredients in a bowl, then add the colouring to the warm water and stir. Now add your coloured water to the dry mix and stir until it's all combined. I then pour this onto a plate, to make it easy for everyone to get stuck in and place little hands or feet into the paint to coat them before transferring them to paper and making prints.

Homemade watercolour paint

FROM SCRATCH

WHAT YOU WILL NEED

5 tbsp warm water
1/3 cup cornflour
Mixing bowl
Spoon
Small bowls
Food colouring

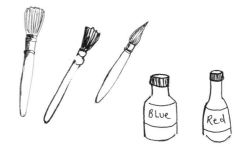

METHOD

When I was having a paint-making session one day in the kitchen, I had a very happy accident that resulted in this silky watercolour paint, and I am so pleased to share it with you here.

Add the warm water to the cornflour in a bowl and stir. It will initially feel almost solid and you have to work through it with the stirring until it loosens up; this is the reason why the water needs to be warm, otherwise you will be there a long time! I then divide the mixture among small bowls and add a few drops of colouring to each. The white of the cornflour means that your end result will be creamy in tone, and this paints onto paper so beautifully, merging like watercolours and blending perfectly. The good news is, it also dries super-fast – 6 minutes to be precise!

Tutti frutti gift wrap

WHAT YOU WILL NEED

Tissue paper or brown paper – a long roll is ideal

Paint

Plate(s)

Selection of fruit and veg, e.g. corn on the cob, strawberries, lemon, orange, apple, red pepper

Kitchen roll

ENGAGED FOR

20 minutes, with fruit prepped beforehand.

POTENTIAL FOR MESS

Paint mess is possible, but lay down a Kraft table-cloth and it will certainly minimize this.

PARENTAL ENJOYMENT

I really love this – it's reminiscent of potato stamping and its results are charming.

GOOD STUFF

Confidence

Creativity

Imagination

Thinking

METHOD

Who wouldn't love a gift presented to them wrapped in handprinted paper? When my daughter and I were playing around with stamps made from carved-out fruit and veg, it occurred to me that we could stamp them onto tissue paper and stock up on some homemade gift wrap. So although this is a very simple activity, I wanted to share it with you because it is so useful and it kept Mabel entertained for a good hour of arty play.

I had never really thought beyond potato stamps, which, like pumpkin carving, include knife skills that are a little too advanced for the toddler age group. Instead I wanted to discover which fruits naturally make the prettiest patterns without too much slicing.

To get started, I lay out all the paper on the table, because once you are in your flow with the stamping it's hard to stop and even better when it's dry and have your wrapping paper on hand!

I put the paint on a big plate or use a few plates of different colours to give some variety – I'd say, let go of the idea that these colours will not get merged and mixed into sludge brown by the end of it! I cut the juicier fruits in half and then we dry them with kitchen roll before Mabel starts stamping; this way the paint stays nice and thick, which keeps the form more distinct.

Corn on the cob can be rolled in the paint then rolled across the paper for a dotted effect. If you have the time, you could perhaps do a first layer, leave it to dry, then roll over the paper again in a different colour to give a double-dotted, 3D effect.

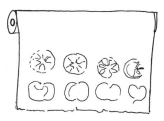

Homemade glue

WHAT YOU WILL NEED

1/4 cup cornflour

Pinch of salt

1/2 cup water

Mixing bowl

Fork, to mix

Saucepan

Heatproof bowl

Wooden spoon

METHOD

I did a lot of experimenting with various recipes to make my own child-friendly glue, and I was pleased to finally land on this one – it dries quickly, is so easy to make and it really, REALLY sticks!

Whisk the cornflour, salt (to help prevent mould) and water in a bowl with a fork until it is a smooth consistency, a little like pancake batter, then pour it into a saucepan and heat very gently, stirring all the time with a wooden spoon, to thicken. Don't take your eyes off the mix because it will suddenly become thick (you will see it go translucent at the edges, which is when you have to take it off the heat). Remove from the heat, pour into a heatproof bowl and stir it until it cools a little. You will end up with what looks like a mass of Pritt stick, which is perfect. Because of its fast-drying quality, this will only keep for a few hours, so always make it just before you need it.

Homemade glaze

FROM SCRATCH

WHAT YOU WILL NEED

Saucepan

Heatproof bowl

Fork

1/4 cup flour

1/2 cup water

Pinch of salt

METHOD

In a saucepan whisk the flour and water together with a fork and add a pinch of salt. When your mixture resembles pancake batter, put your saucepan onto a gentle heat. Take it off the heat as soon as the consistency starts to thicken and decant into a heatproof bowl.

Pressed-flower jars

WHAT YOU WILL NEED

Loose parts: petals/dried flowers/leaves/grasses (see page 22)

Glass jars

Saucepan

Whisk

Paintbrush

Homemade glaze (see page 61)

ENGAGED FOR

We pre-made the glaze which took us 5 or 6 minutes; we had pre-pressed flowers and putting them together took us around 15 minutes. For you, this will depend on how much you want to decorate the jars and how long your children can concentrate with a creating activity.

POTENTIAL FOR MESS

A little bit of glue mess but with the homemade glue recipe in this book, it's easy to wash off hands, table and clothing.

PARENTAL ENJOYMENT

A perfect gift, or tea-light holder – I don't think this activity should be strictly reserved for children.

GOOD STUFF

Bonding

Confidence

Creativity

Imagination

Nature

Speaking

Thinking

METHOD

I think these make the most beautiful, simple gifts for grandparents or friends with messages or trinkets inside, but they are equally charming with a little tea light candle in (battery-powered or real, depending on what you prefer or the level of supervision available if you're keeping these!). Collect together some petals, dried flowers, leaves or grasses (the flatter the better, or press them between books for a few hours prior to use) and a few used, clean glass jars. If, like me, you cannot bear to throw away any glass jars, perhaps choose the least pickley-smelling ones!

Your kids can then gift these or use them as pretty upcycled tea light holders – the glow of 'candle' light and the floral silhouettes projected are as enchanting as you'd expect.

Get your kids to choose the natural loose parts they want to stick on the jars, then get them to paste the glaze onto the jars using a paintbrush, layering the loose parts on top, then painting the glaze over them. The glaze will dry with a frosted effect and remain secure enough for the decorations to stay in place.

NOTES, DRAWINGS, INSPIRATION

NOTES, DRAWINGS, INSPIRATION

NOTES, DRAWINGS, INSPIRATION

NOTES, DRAWINGS, INSPIRATION

NOTES, DRAWINGS, INSPIRATION

'Joy, feeling one's own value, being appreciated and loved by others, feeling useful and capable of production are all factors of enormous value for the human soul.'

Maria Montessori

Water Babies

Both of my daughters were born in water, slowly and calmly emerging from warm, womb-like birthing pools (thank you, hypnobirthing!). Water, for me, was the place where I was most able to relax, let go and lean into the sensations of labour, my body weightless. Perhaps their manner of arrival in the world, through this watery portal from the similarly supportive womb, is why both of my children, like many other babies and toddlers, turn tranquil at the sight of water.

A 'colourless, transparent, odourless liquid' are the unremarkable words used to describe water, which is so remarkable. It is our most vital, life-giving, natural resource and 'the driving force of nature', according to Leonardo da Vinci.

It is no surprise then that water is also the most versatile and open-ended component to free and creative play. Used for bathing, paddling, mixing, squirting, scrubbing, bubbling, swirling, swishing, pouring or scooping, water is a sensory pool of exploration. Whether it's my youngest daughter Peggy, watching in amazement as water trickles from a tap, reaching for it and experiencing new sensations on her tiny hands, or Mabel with her 'Magic Water', her imagination running wild as she paints the patio with a brush and cup of H_2O, watching quietly as the shapes and patterns that she's just created disappear, like magic. It transfixes them.

Looking back at my own childhood, I was often involved in water-based projects, from making potions with water and crushed petals, proud of my back-garden apothecary, to using bin liners (nowadays we'd be more eco!) to line homemade ponds, in the process destroying my mother's flower beds and never achieving the frogspawn habitat I longed for. Even now, as an adult, I adore the feeling of dangling my toes in the water at a river's edge or having a long hot bath – on those rare nights when the babies are asleep before ridiculous o'clock. Equally, I find the swaying of an ocean or rhythmic flow of a fountain totally mesmerizing. It certainly distracts my mind and soothes me when I need it to.

In this chapter, you will find ideas for enhancing water play with your kids that are both calming and invigorating, dependent on their moods and what state you want them to be in by the end of each activity – whether it's a sleep-inducing bath-salt recipe to aid the transition to bedtime, or, my personal favourite, 'Squishy Soap', which is the five-minute miracle cure for bad moods, playdates and hand hygiene. There is something for most occasions within this chapter, so enter into it with a free-flowing curiosity and untamed enthusiasm for all things aquatic!

Bath crayons

WHAT YOU WILL NEED

1 soap bar

Cheese grater

3 bowls

Poster paint

Spoon

Warm water

Ice cube tray

POTENTIAL FOR MESS

Certainly my experimental process and recipe testing for these crayons was painfully messy (I took one for the team, for sure), but hopefully I've honed this into a compact and doable activity that can be enjoyed during bathtime and all evidence washed down right away in the shower or tub!

ENGAGED FOR

The making was fast as I prepped and grated the soap in advance. We mixed it all together pretty swiftly – because it hardens as you stir. The crayons will need to freeze for 4 hours – preferably overnight – before use.

PARENTAL ENJOYMENT

Anything that makes getting them clean less of a struggle surely earns some parental points!

GOOD STUFF

Bonding

Creativity

Imagination

Listening

Self-care

Senses

METHOD

Where do I even start with this one? I tried out several variations of bath crayon recipes one morning when both children were at my feet, one walking and the other making wobbly attempts. I was naive in thinking that getting everyone into the shower to test out the recently frozen bath crayons was a good idea. It certainly showed me which type the true winner was (i.e. the bath crayons that caused the LEAST mess, but drew well and held their shape the longest). I will elaborate on the star recipe shortly, but not before briefly painting a picture (!) of how the first experimentation went.

I tried making a set of crayons using food colouring and a liquid soap/water mix . . . well, as you can imagine, these not only melted very quickly but were also slimy and the colour like a volcanic eruption of deep inky stain. Thankfully, I had at least closed the bathroom door before letting a toddler loose with these little nubs of destruction (nubs being all they were, having quickly lost all sense of the

vessel they had been frozen in) but hands were covered, PJs were covered and little Peggy, nude as the day, was also covered. I tried to grab at some toilet roll to clean it out of the tile grout, which had not long ago been bright white, before literally having to pull on the shower curtain to stop myself from slipping over babies and paint splatters, then in a clichéd, slapstick moment, the curtain was pulled from its rings and the three of us tumbled into a little pile. Mabel was unimpressed that I quickly had to put an end to the experimenting, as she was deeply into the messy nubs, while Peggy was left amazed by the whole thing. I just felt regretful and bothered about the tile grout and wondered how long it would be before it was stained forever.

That said, three absolute gems followed, so let's not rush off and cancel this completely before explaining how to SUCCESSFULLY make mess-free, fun, slip-proof bath crayons . . .

I prepped this activity by grating a bar of soap until I had about 1 cup's worth, then divided that up into three bowls. I added a tablespoon of poster paint to each bowl (I chose green, red and orange) and then got Mabel to stir it. I asked her to keep stirring while I added a tablespoon of warm water to each. You should then have a sort of soapy putty forming – you will see the grated soap bits too – so keep stirring until the colour is combined.

Grab your ice cube tray and ask your little one to push the mixture into the cubes. Pop this into the freezer overnight (or if making this in the daytime, give it at least 4 hours before they are bathtime ready), then pop them out as needed.

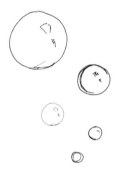

Squishy soap

WHAT YOU WILL NEED

1/2 cup cornflour

Mixing bowl

4 tbsp liquid soap

4 tsp cooking oil

Spoon

Jar with lid

ENGAGED FOR

About 5 minutes to make and weeks of play.

PARENTAL ENJOYMENT

HUGE, because it is so effective. Simple, natural and fascinating.

GOOD STUFF

Bonding

Creativity

Listening

Self-care

Senses

POTENTIAL FOR MESS

There is a moment, when you tip the mixture onto the work surface, that seems a bit wayward, scattered and scary, BUT it redeems itself within seconds, trust me!

METHOD

Bathtime play was the main inspiration for this activity; however, the result has way exceeded my hopes and dreams and is now used to encourage hand-washing regularly, water play outside and has even on occasion managed to defuse unbelievable tantrums. It is the miraculous . . . SQUISHY SOAP!

I don't know if you remember the packets of squishy soap (or was it called putty?) from The Body Shop in the 1990s, wrapped up like sweets, smelling of pineapple – it's making me swoon just to reminisce on it now. Well, this is like that. Except we know exactly what goes into it and it's safe, natural and so easy to make it will blow your mind.

As with Play Dough (see page 45), I decided to measure out my ingredients before allowing them into the hands of my toddler – as this removes any possibility of overpouring and it means the activity would hold her attention span successfully. Of course, if you have older children, do let them get into the weights and measures as they will enjoy that scientific element. So, I put the cornflour into a bowl, then the wet ingredients followed before I handed over to Mabel and let her stir until the consistency was like a 'more powdery' and oily play dough. I then, SHOCK HORROR, poured it out onto the table and let her mush it about. I had a go myself, gathering the stray bits of mixture into the surprisingly silky ball that was forming, then kneaded it a few times.

After a tussle over who got to play with it first, we were left with a remarkable moisturizing, play-dough-but-not, bubbly ball of mouldable soap. This is now offered up at bathtime, after playing in the garden and before lunch, and sometimes just with a big bowl of water and towel on the kitchen floor, which honestly settles any challenging emotions.

'Do you reckon you might like to play with the squishy soap now?' – I hear myself exclaim, more times than I thought possible.

Pop it into a lidded jar between uses, and ENJOY!

Bath paint

WHAT YOU WILL NEED

Small bowl

1 tbsp cornflour

1 tbsp liquid soap

1 tbsp warm water

Colouring

Paint brush

Jar with lid (for storage)

(Makes a small batch for 1 bath)

POTENTIAL FOR MESS

Messy fun BUT you couldn't be in a better place to wash everything off afterwards.

ENGAGED FOR

Minutes to prepare, and it will make bathtimes last that little bit longer.

PARENTAL ENJOYMENT

It is so easy to make and it really helps to create a bonding bathtime experience.

GOOD STUFF

Bonding

Creativity

Imagination

Self-care

Senses

METHOD

Bathtime for us is a thing: a ritual, a time of bonding and joy. Anything that adds to this is welcomed, and we have used this recipe for bath paint over and over again. It is used to depict elements of the day, Pictionary-style guessing games and general messy fun in a wash-down environment.

The first time I made bath paint, it was a thick gloop of bright orange cornflour that I could barely run a brush through. That's not the worst part of it – it was orange because I decided to use turmeric as my natural colouring. My unassuming husband was on bathtime duty that night and I handed him the pot of dye, I mean paint . . . and told him to 'go wild and have fun'. I assured him it didn't matter if it went on the walls as it would come off . . . Yeah, right. The condition was that he reported back on the great success of the paint. Well, I heard a shout through to me after

about twenty minutes, and when I opened the door, I was almost blinded by the glare of turmeric covering their faces, bodies, the bath, the walls and the floor. He was quick to inform me, it wasn't coming off!

So after a lot of scrubbing, a good dose of heavy-duty bathroom cleaner (left on to soak for 24 hours) and two tangoed family members for a good few days, I decided to try again and quickly crossed off 'turmeric' as a possible colourant, saving all of you from the same disaster!

I successfully produced a good, washable bath paint on the a second attempt . . . so to do this get a small bowl and mix the cornflour with the liquid soap and warm water until you have a smooth consistency. Using warm water helps keep the cornflour/ soap mix loose and smooth. I used a tiny drop of food colouring at this point which thankfully is completely user friendly, but equally you can use natural colourings made from fruits or vegetables, adding a small concentrated amount to your paint mix and stirring until combined. The sneaky secret here is that this paint also works well on glass and it comes off in just one wipe – no scraping, no damage. So if you would like to get creative on your windows at home, this is the one for you.

The bath paint will last a couple of days in a jar with a lid on, stored in a cool place.

Comforting bath bundle

WHAT YOU WILL NEED

1 cup rolled oats

1 cup ground oats

½ cup dried chamomile

2 lengths of twine (about 15cm each)

3 small bowls

A teaspoon

2 squares of thin cloth (e.g. cheesecloth, or muslin), 15cm x 15cm, or thereabouts

1 large cookie cutter

POTENTIAL FOR MESS

Using the cookie cutter for guidance, by getting them to spoon the mixture into the centre of it, will help reduce mess and spillage. As with the Sleepy Bath Salts (see page 85), I'd suggest using a tray when making this.

ENGAGED FOR

About 5–10 minutes of gentle, focused play.

PARENTAL ENJOYMENT

Calm, peaceful and satisfying. Quick and focused, meaning it requires almost no time at all set aside from your day. It can also be a lovely add-on just before bathtime.

GOOD STUFF

Bonding

Creativity

Listening

Nurture

Self-care

Senses

METHOD

Along with our Sleepy Bath Salts, we made these oat bundles for a skin-calming bathtime treat. There are so many benefits of using oats in a baby's bath, including being anti-inflammatory so it helps calm rashes and itching, and having soothing and moisturizing properties, so it's perfect for cold days and eczema-prone skin. I had some leftover cheesecloth (loose woven cotton) from making homemade bath bundles for family and friends at Christmas, so we used this, cut into squares, to hold our oat mixture. You could also use an old cloth or T-shirt, anything that liquid will be able to get through without releasing the mixture out with it.

As with all the activities using measured ingredients, put everything in small bowls first so that you and your child can focus on combining and mixing rather than pouring the entire bag of salt all over the place. I lay a square of cloth on a tray surrounded by the ingredients and offer a teaspoon to my daughter to start creating her oaty bundle. The first time, I realized after the first few spoonfuls of ground oats that the mixture was not staying in the centre, where I'd intended it to be so that I could fold up the sides to contain it. Keeping the mixture in the centre makes tying it up so much easier as well as making this a less messy activity, so I quickly opened the kitchen cupboard (before Mabel got overexcited at this potential for mess) and found a large circular cookie cutter, which then became the guiding tool and was a great success. I put the cutter onto the centre of the cloth and I asked Mabel to fill the middle of the cutter – we managed the rest of this activity with no scattered oats. Use the teaspoon to stir each time more ingredients are added, then when you have filled the cookie cutter to the top, take it away carefully before bringing the sides of the cloth into one bunch and tying with twine (as on p82). This is a free and flowing activity and it doesn't matter what goes in or when; take your time and have a go by adding some of the suggested dried flowers at the end of this recipe.

Once it is in the bath being used like a sponge, you can immediately feel the effect of its hydrating contents as it clouds the water like the beautifying milk baths of Cleopatra.

A friend noted that this is actually the perfect homemade gift for a toddler to give a beloved family member in need of a bit of pampering, so including some variations that could be used in place of, or alongside, the chamomile.

Using oats in the bath is a traditional method of calming the unbearable itch of chicken pox. Put the oatmeal

directly into the bath water and let it soak for 15–20 minutes before your child gets in then pat them dry gently afterwards with a clean towel.

OTHER IDEAS FOR THE BATH BUNDLES . . .

Dried rosebuds or rose petals for a beautiful fragrance.

Dried lavender for tranquility and relaxation.

Dried calendula flowers (marigolds) for skin-calming and hydrating.

Sleepy bath salts

WHAT YOU WILL NEED

2 cups Epsom bath salts

1 cup dried lavender

A spoon

Jam jar/sugar shaker

Small bowls

Tray

POTENTIAL FOR MESS

Try to keep the ingredients on a big tray, as there will inevitably be mess when you are asking a child (especially a toddler) to spoon grains of anything into a jar. If you don't have a tray, a baking tray or plate will do.

ENGAGED FOR

We took 5–10 minutes making this – spooning, mixing, shaking and smelling.

PARENTAL ENJOYMENT

I loved seeing Mabel engage in something in a relaxed way. Given that I have already expressed my love of creating lotions and potions, this was a perfect experience. If they decide to throw the lot in the bath, so be it – you know that the process of making this has been beautiful. Just don't let them drink the water!

GOOD STUFF

Bonding

Creativity

Listening

Nurture

Senses

Thinking

METHOD

This is the perfect wind-down evening activity for you to try with your two-plus year-olds. I personally enjoy making my own bath salts, body oils and scrubs, and having done some research into child-safe and family friendly remedies, I decided to end a long week with this calming activity before a Friday bathtime.

Putting your ingredients into kid-proof vessels whilst you are out of sight is a good way to start any 'potion making'. I often present Mabel with a tray of items that we can use and this introduces her to the idea that we are going to sit together and do a focused activity.

I set out a little bowl of each of the ingredients with a spoon and I told Mabel that we were going to make a lovely treat that she could use in her bath later. I got her to smell the dried lavender and told her that this would to help her feel sleepy. I kept the lighting low and we used hushed voices, as I asked her to help me by mixing the bath salts and lavender and stirring as she went – hushed voices kept it low energy so that it remained a calm activity.

All going well so far, I thought, as Mabel and I carried the precious sugar shaker (that I had found in our kitchen cupboard earlier that day) up to the bathroom ready for its moment of glory. Mabel was thrilled at the thought that she had made this mixture herself and we were getting to use it, so I gave her the shaker to sprinkle it delicately into the bath. Well, that's when the shaker got thrown, FULL PELT, into the water. It took me a moment to get over feeling deeply annoyed and defeated, but her joy was untarnished and I had to quickly bring myself to fish it out, before the whole bath was contaminated with salt and disappointment. The fact is, she had the best night's sleep she'd had for months. The creative process had been a total success and once I got over the rest of the batch being unusable, I was able to appreciate the quiet collaboration, and later the undisturbed sleep!

I must add here that we have since made these sleepy bath salts several times and I can confirm that, with my wits about me, there has been no further sugar-shaker-slinging . . .

Bubble bath for toys

WHAT YOU WILL NEED

Bowl of warm soapy water

(Waterproof) toys

Tea towel

Old toothbrush, nail brush, sponges (optional)

ENGAGED FOR

20–25 minutes – this is a very easy activity to set up and not one you'd necessarily think of right away.

POTENTIAL FOR MESS

Lay down the towel and encourage a quiet environment, for focused, calm play.

PARENTAL ENJOYMENT

As I write this, I am thinking about setting this up for my daughter right now, who is having a 'sick day' and off nursery. It is a really lovely, easy activity and you will appreciate how much kids love to lend a helping hand.

GOOD STUFF

Creativity

Imagination

Nurturing

Senses

Thinking

METHOD

With a weaning baby in tow, we are never short of toys that need a bath. This has become a staple, rather helpful, and a little bit messy activity in our household. We make up a big bowl of warm soapy water and then give our (waterproof) toys a lovely relaxing bubble bath. Each is given the care and dedication that one would expect at any top spa!

Lay a tea towel next to the bowl so that the toys can lie out to dry after their valet. We often use our small animal figurines when we are playing in the garden, in the soil, so this is a perfect antidote to that mess.

Magic water

WHAT YOU WILL NEED

1 small bowl water

Paintbrush

METHOD

This really is joy in its simplest form. A small bowl of water and a paintbrush (that is all). A wonderful thing. It's a minimal-mess activity that takes seconds to prepare and will occupy your toddler for a surprising amount of time – certainly long enough to make yourself a cup of tea and drink it whilst it's still hot, anyway! Painting with water on the kitchen cupboards and windows really is MAGIC and the ideal exercise for their wild imaginations.

Coloured foam

WHAT YOU WILL NEED

Cupcake tray
Food colouring
Shaving foam
(non-scented, for
sensitive skin is best)
Spoon or paintbrush

ENGAGED FOR

5 minutes, before the
tray ended up in the bath,
but the fun continued
for the duration of bath
time – with soapy foamy
illustrations all over the
place. So in total a good
25 minutes of shaving
foam fun!

POTENTIAL FOR MESS

For bathtubs. We started
with it outside the bath
in a cupcake tray, but once
the excitement started
to grow with the colour
changing foam, we moved
it into a contained 'wash
down' space.

PARENTAL ENJOYMENT

This was so easy and really
had great results, so I'd say
this was a hit with me, too.

GOOD STUFF

Creativity
Imagination
Self-care
Senses

METHOD

Grab a cupcake tray, put a drop of food
colouring in the bottom of each mould
and then a squirt of shaving foam on
the top. Give your little one a spoon
or paintbrush and when they start to
mix, they will gasp in delight at the
expanding, colour-changing foam. You
will have brightly coloured foamy fun.
It paints well in the bath tub, too!

Frozen paint pops

WHAT YOU WILL NEED

Food colouring/ kids' paint

Ice cube tray

Water

Lollipop sticks

Paper

Kitchen roll

Small bowl

ENGAGED FOR

5 minutes to make and 10 minutes of play, before they start to melt!

POTENTIAL FOR MESS

I made a lot of mess trying out various quantities of colouring and water, but I've arrived at this recipe that is easy and – if you take full control of the food colouring – a relatively mess-free process. Melted paint pops will leave brightly coloured puddles, so keep some kitchen roll to hand, or perhaps a bowl to rest them in.

PARENTAL ENJOYMENT

Moments of horror when I see the paint pops heading towards the mouth, mistaken for lollies, but quickley diverted and great fun all-round.

GOOD STUFF

Confidence

Creativity

Imagination

Listening

Senses

METHOD

I wasn't sure what would work better when I was testing frozen paint pops; would it be the trusty food colouring (a pantry staple), or perhaps I could just freeze shop-bought kid-friendly paint? Well, they each created completely different effects, so I am including both of these as options, depending on your mood.

It is the same process either way. To try this out yourself, put a few drops of food colouring or paint into the bottom of the compartments of an ice cube tray, top up with water and, using a lollipop stick or the end of a teaspoon, gently stir until the mixture is completely combined. Put the tray into the freezer and 45 minutes later

place your lollipop sticks into the centre of each block, as they should be able to stand up by this point. Leave the blocks to freeze for another couple of hours then pop them out, onto a plate, ready to use.

I was surprised at how bright and inky the food colouring pops ended up – creating gorgeous streaks of vibrant colour on sheets of paper, reminiscent of the famous Inkblot tests.

The frozen paint pops were a much more hardy product and drew onto the paper like crayon – the lighter strokes were ideal for longer-lasting outdoor summer play!

Sensory water play

WHAT YOU WILL NEED

Large mixing bowl/ deep baking tray

1 litre water

Loose parts (see below and page 22)

ENGAGED FOR

Endless . . . this is one of my favourite activities when I am tired, when I haven't got it in me to source materials; once you start putting a sensory table together it definitely sparks your creativity, even when you thought that it was a losing battle.

POTENTIAL FOR MESS

Water-mess but so much joy to be had in the process. Have hand towels at the ready and take it outside if possible.

PARENTAL ENJOYMENT

I love seeing my girls engaged in sensory water play. They absolutely love it and whether they are playing together or independently, it occupies a good chunk of TV-free time and feels good for everyone's soul.

GOOD STUFF

Confidence

Creativity

Emotion

Imagination

Senses

Speaking

Thinking

METHOD

Both of our daughters adore sensory water play, which is exploration for their senses as well as a perfect quick fix for hot children in the summer months. Developmentally, playing with water is beneficial for coordination and creative thinking. It can also be calming or energizing depending on what style of play you go for. Water play is a chance to explore new sensations, so I have listed here a few ideas to start with that we have tried and tested and come back to over again.

All three suggestions here require you to fill a mixing bowl or deep baking tray with cool water before adding your loose parts. If you are able to do this outside, obviously any spillages will dry up after you've finished playing; however, when we do this inside I put down a towel and get the girls to play on it in their designated area!

Refresh and Invigorate

WHAT YOU WILL NEED

6 cucumber slices

4 lemon slices

2 lemon wedges

A lemon squeezer

Wooden spoon

Ice cubes (on hot days)

Cut slices of cucumber and lemon, and also some lemon wedges, and put them into the water. Optional tools for this would be a lemon squeezer and a wooden spoon for mixing as well as hands, to squeeze, juice and mix the lemons and cucumber in the water. On hot days, ice cubes can be added for extra cooling!

By the Seaside

WHAT YOU WILL NEED

1 drop blue food colouring
1 drop green food colouring
Seashells
Sea life figurines or bath toys
Sieve/fork

Calming Lavender

WHAT YOU WILL NEED

1 drop red food colouring

1 drop blue food colouring

Fresh lavender or dried lavender buds

Ladle

Mixing spoon

2 cups

If you have collected shells that are sitting untouched from last year's summer holiday, this is a great opportunity to seek them out. Put the drops of blue and green food colouring into the water and add the shells – we also use sea life figurines. Get a small sieve or a fork and now go fishing for your items, one at a time. This is a great activity for focus and holiday nostalgia.

Put a drop of red and a drop of blue food colouring into the water and mix until you have a light purple colour. Add some freshly picked or dried lavender buds to the water. Find a ladle and mixing spoon from the kitchen and use them to scoop and pour the water into cups.

Bubble painting

WHAT YOU WILL NEED

1 tbsp washing-up liquid

1 tbsp paint

1 tbsp water

Shallow dish/bowl

Spoon

Paper straw

Paper

ENGAGED FOR

15 minutes

POTENTIAL FOR MESS

Mess as standard for a painty, watery activity. Use a tray and all the spillages will most likely stay in one place.

PARENTAL ENJOYMENT

Very beautiful result here, with coloured bubble patterns on the paper. We are building a stock to make into cards. Reminiscent of marbling ink.

GOOD STUFF

Creativity

Imagination

Senses

Speaking

METHOD

Put the washing-up liquid, paint and water into a bowl and stir until it is all mixed together and you can start to see bubbles appearing. Now make all your child's bubble-blowing dreams come true by asking them to blow bubbles into the mixture (but not to suck in!) through the straw. You will start to see the most fantastic bubbles appearing, all growing on top of one another until it's like a massive hive of bubbles. At this point you can put your paper gently on top of the bubbles. I usually have three colour mixes on the go at the same time in separate bowls, so you can layer the popping pattern by moving the sheet of paper from one bowl of colour to the next. Turning over your page will reveal your colourful bubbles captured forever . . .

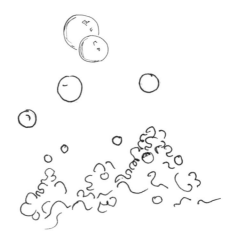

NOTES, DRAWINGS, INSPIRATION

NOTES, DRAWINGS, INSPIRATION

NOTES, DRAWINGS, INSPIRATION

NOTES, DRAWINGS, INSPIRATION

'Creativity is inventing, experimenting, growing, taking risks, breaking rules, making mistakes, and having fun.'

Mary Lou Cook

Force of Nature

As I write this book, it is a warm summer and our household consists of a teething baby and a toddler exercising willpower while learning all about her own sense of independence. There is a lot of juggling, a lot of crying and a lot of hot, frustrated individuals (myself and husband included).

On one of the long, late-night sessions the other evening, induced by sore gums, I decided to go and sit outside with Peggy, who by this point (11pm) was beyond tired and uncomfortable in her own skin, dribbling and gnawing at the corner of a pyjama sleeve. The minute I took her outside into the cool night air, the crying stopped . . . immediately. She was sat in my arms and the tension dropped right through her entire body and she just made a long, happy gurgle, as if to tell me, thank goodness you finally knew where I wanted to be. The same applies when we are in some negotiation with Mabel, the indoor space can become an enclosing pressure on us all as we let her express EVERY feeling. A swift change of scenery and blast of fresh air usually provides that much-needed energy shift and everything seems to settle in her much more quickly, distracted now as she is by the ants, watching a plane fly over or by digging her hands in soil.

There is such strong evidence that daily outdoor play for children is not only beneficial to their physical health

but also to their mental well-being – reducing stress, strengthening their immune systems, keeping them active, stimulating their senses, and nurturing their creativity, curiosity and problem-solving abilities. As well as the essential free outdoor play that Angela Hanscom writes about so wonderfully in her book *Balanced and Barefoot*, she also reminds us that 'virtually everything that can be done indoors can also be done outdoors . . . even ordinary tasks such as eating and bathing can happen outside for a fun, enriching, and memorable experience'. I know a lot of my own sacred memories from childhood are based on being outdoors, like the nostalgia for my grandparents' garden on summer evenings in Edinburgh, or the hours spent in my much-loved den at home, decorating it with old carpet and rhododendron petals; autumnal walks with my godmother, finding conkers and drying them out on her Aga, or finding the best slopes on snowy days to toboggan down with my mum, dressed head to toe in my sister's hand-me-down ski gear.

The possibilities are limitless for how nature and outdoor space can work for your creative play time with your children, and within this chapter I have collated a few ideas that I hope will inspire you to connect with your natural surroundings and use everything that they offer you, whatever the weather.

Nature crowns

WHAT YOU WILL NEED

Craft paper/
paper shopping bags

Scissors

Petals/flowers/leaves

Paints, pencils, crayons
(optional)

Homemade
glue (see
page 60) or
Pritt stick

POTENTIAL FOR MESS

Minimal. All the bits and
pieces of flora can be
stuck onto the crown, so
nothing gets left behind!

ENGAGED FOR

About 30 minutes inside
or outside – dependent on
the weather.

PARENTAL ENJOYMENT

I felt very pleased to have
repurposed the multitude
of paper shopping bags
that I had. I was then
inspired to cut up some
more and have an extra
stock of drawing and craft
paper to hand. The crowns
were a joy to make for
all of us and they looked
adorable, too.

GOOD STUFF

Bonding

Creativity

Imagination

Nature

Thinking

METHOD

One warm spring morning I was trying to think of a gentle activity to do in the garden. Flowers were coming into bloom, and with an Easter party a few days away, Mabel was in the mood for fancy dress and celebration. I'd seen lots of paper cut-out bunny ears cropping up on Instagram around this time, painted or made from coloured paper, but we felt like being a little more regal (plus the only paper I could find wouldn't actually stand upright like  bunny ears). Luckily, despite a lack of suitable card, I had a bunch of brown-paper shopping bags that were keen to be made into crowns.

I cut open the bags so they were completely flat, then drew out the shape of a crown, adding a little extra length to ensure I could stick it together securely later. I did the cutting – we aren't there yet with the scissors – and then I handed over to Mabel.

We had gone around picking lots of bits and bobs from around the garden, so we had bowls of petals, grass, daisies and seedlings at the ready for decoration. I was working on a miniature crown for Peggy and used some watercolour paints as 'round jewels', then sprinkled the flora onto glued areas (much like you'd do with glitter), blowing off the excess. Mabel was doing the same with hers and, as always, going in hard with the black paint, which was actually a beautiful contrast to the bright purple wisteria flowers she later added.

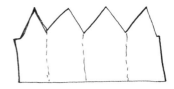

I let the crowns dry flat for an hour, then I added a line of glue at the ends and brought them round to meet, holding the glued line securely for a moment until I was sure it would stick.

This was a such a lovely, simple activity, which just used things we had around the house and garden, meaning that there was no frantic searching for big pieces of paper, no glittery spillages – just an adorable little King or Queen at the end of it.

Twig and twine worry dolls

WHAT YOU WILL NEED

Twigs

Twine/wool

Scissors

POTENTIAL FOR MESS

This is the perfect activity for those days when you don't fancy cleaning up paint splatters or water splashes.

ENGAGED FOR

Around 20–30 minutes.

PARENTAL ENJOYMENT

A wonderful group or family activity on a rainy Sunday around the kitchen table.

GOOD STUFF

Bonding

Confidence

Creativity

Emotion

Imagination

Nature

Speaking

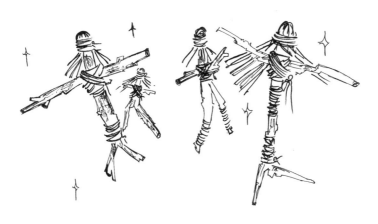

METHOD

Shall we do a family activity? I asked my husband one very windy Sunday afternoon during the summer holidays. I was feeling moon sand or play dough vibes, but unlike me my husband does not gravitate towards the slimy, sticky, all-you-can-eat creative experiences with our mess-loving little girls.

Stick Man is a favourite film in our household, and because of our love of the Forest School method (which focuses on outdoor learning, nature-based craft and free-form play), we were familiar with the idea of making our own stick people, so Russell suggested we do just that. In this case we decided to elaborate and use twine, not only to bind the sticks but clothe them in a mix of bright colours. Then we used a bunch of wool strands at the top of each upright stick, tied round and carefully trimmed for exceptional 1980s-style haircuts.

Setting this up was easy, as there were branches flying every which way in the wind, so I carefully collected some. I had twine and a ball of wool in our craft cupboard already, and as I try to do for most activities, I did the cutting in advance so that we didn't

need to do any at the table, keeping the activity scissor-free. You can either choose twigs that already appear to have arms and legs, then wrap the coloured yarn as you please to brighten your figurines, or if you need to bind sticks together for the same effect, I'd suggest making a cross with them, then weaving the twine over and under the meeting point several times, then pulling it tight before tying it to secure. You should now have a frame to work with and personalize.

We made our own family in twig form that day, and because of the resemblance (albeit more rustic) to traditional Mayan 'worry dolls', we decided to endow our twig family with the same responsibilities: being listeners, confidantes and emotional tools (minus putting them under the pillow!). Your little ones can find comfort in their trusted homemade twig friends by whispering their worries, fears and anxieties to them, then taking them outside and, holding them carefully, asking that the wind blow all their worries away.

Wild weaving

WHAT YOU WILL NEED

4 strong sticks

4 short pieces of string/twine

1 long piece of string/twine

Natural loose parts

POTENTIAL FOR MESS

None!

ENGAGED FOR

Around 15 minutes to make the structure for weaving, then some more time spent on a walk, threading discoveries into it.

PARENTAL ENJOYMENT

Teaching a toddler to tie string to secure twigs is not totally straightforward and despite trying to teach Mabel a couple of times (she is not yet attempting shoe laces), I decided that this bit is better for the grown-ups to do. I was incredibly satisfied with having created such a structure with 4 sticks, I must say, and had a real spring in my step when we went off into the wilds to start weaving our magic.

GOOD STUFF

Adventure

Bonding

Creativity

Listening

Nature

METHOD

Weaving is another one of the hand-based crafts that are good for relaxation and mindfulness; I've seen it said of weaving, 'busy hands, quiet minds', because of the calming effect it has as a hobby and de-stressing experience. This is a wonderful activity to practise with your children for a bit of autumnal calm, and the beauty of it is that you can take your loom (apparatus for weaving) on nature hunts and mindful walks gathering flowers, weeds, grasses and feathers as you go.

Begin by finding strong sticks that are all around the same length, then create the outline of a square with them – this will be your loom. Secure it by tying the short pieces of twine around the crossed-over points on each of the four corners. Criss-cross over these points with the twine, then tie it at the back once you are happy that it feels like a strong hold. Now take the long piece of twine and tie it around one of the corners, then over to the opposite side, wrapping it around the opposite sides and back and forth until you have a web of twine.

This is now ready for gathering with a spirit of traditional craft adventure. When you come across a perfect bit for your creation (we did well to avoid a big clump of dog hair being woven in on a recent trip to a park), thread it over and under the pieces of twine until it runs through the loom. The next treasure will be woven alongside that one, and so on, until your loom is filled!

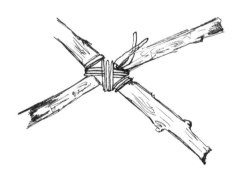

Nature paintbrushes

WHAT YOU WILL NEED

Twigs

Leaves, feathers, reeds, grasses, flowers

Twine

Scissors

Paint

Plates (optional)

Kraft paper – preferably a roll

POTENTIAL FOR MESS

With all painting there is potential for mess, but if you stretch out a big Kraft roll of paper in the garden on a sunny day or on the kitchen floor, you will be able to manage this with minimal clear-up.

ENGAGED FOR

About 25–30 minutes, with a little additional time to gather your materials outside.

PARENTAL ENJOYMENT

Hunting and gathering is always a lovely joint activity, and to be able to make something crafty with the scavenged items feels fun and satisfying.

GOOD STUFF

Bonding

Thinking

Listening

Creativity

Nature

Imagination

Senses

METHOD

I have become obsessed with seeing natural debris as potential for arts and crafts. Wherever I go, I end up with a collection of twigs, leaves and petals, as if to ignore them would mean missing out on some breakthrough creative project.

Once when we did this activity we ended up with a thorny twig in the mix, but luckily it was spotted before it did any damage; we called it 'the ouchy brush' and swiftly put it aside. Other than rogue rose stems, the scope for what can be used to paint with or 'mark make' is pretty great.

Collect together your twigs (these will act as the brush handles) and out of the selection you have, choose the strongest and straightest, as this will ensure the brushes are sturdy. Now gather up leaves, or select a few interesting, unusual-looking flowers or grasses, and bind them with twine to the top of your brush handles, so the foliage is overhanging enough that it could be used to paint with. It may be necessary to wrap the twine several times to hold each brush head securely, then tie it in a knot.

We pour the paint onto plates as it's easier when using peculiar-shaped brushes to have a wider surface area to work with, then we roll out the Kraft paper on a flat surface if we are doing table-top/ground work, or stick it up along a fence/wall. Using a large canvas or roll of paper allows for the most impressive strokes, stamps and patterns, and limits the off-page work causing too much destruction. If you have leftover bits that you didn't use for your brushes, you could suggest trying out floral or leafy stamps on the paper, too. Dip them in the paint until they are covered (the most textured side facing down), then put them straight onto the paper, patting them down before delicately peeling them off.

The thing about these nature paintbrushes and stamps is that rather than achieving accurate portraits or landscapes, they teach us (or remind us!) about the beauty of mark-making, using tools that can found anywhere and are accessible to anyone!

During this activity you can talk about what the brush strokes are doing on the paper, what they look like and how it feels to use leaves to paint with. Engaging with your kids like this exercises everyone's imagination, and harnessing nature always creates the most wonderful artists.

(Cold weather) bird feeder

WHAT YOU WILL NEED

Seed mix, e.g. hemp, linseed, chia, sunflower and pumpkin seeds

Fruit and nut mix, e.g. orange peel, flaked and ground almonds, macadamia and cashew nuts (as appropriate for your child's age and allergies)

Jam jar (370g)

3 tbsp coconut oil

Cupcake tray

Mixing bowl

Wooden spoon

Pencil

Twine

Scissors

POTENTIAL FOR MESS

There is the potential for mess during the mixing stage, of course, but as with all cooking or baking activities, you can prepare by wearing aprons, putting down a table cover, or working on this in the garden – feed the birds with the spillage while you work!

ENGAGED FOR

The time taken to mix, fill and hang, but checking on the bird feeders will also become a thing and can be incorporated into outdoor play in the weeks to come.

PARENTAL ENJOYMENT

I personally enjoy anything that involves nature and recipes, and this is easy to do, with satisfying results. It's also natural, eco-friendly and KIND. Remember, when the weather is cold and food is limited, birds will appreciate the extra bit of help. It feels good to take care of wildlife.

GOOD STUFF

Listening

Creativity

Nature

Care for animals

METHOD

To make your seed, fruit and nut mixes, get a tablespoon of whatever you can get your hands on in the pantry, or try my tested mixes above, which went down very well with the birds in our garden. For the orange peel, I simply cut tiny strips, but equally you could grate a little into the mix. Fill an old jam jar (I often use old jam jars for quantity measuring; the ones I use have a capacity of 370g) with the chosen mix and then prepare your coconut oil.

Grown-ups: put 3 tablespoons of coconut oil into a pan and melt it on the stove. When it's melted, pour it into a mixing bowl along with your jar of seeds and stir with a wooden spoon – remember, it will be hot! When you've given it a stir, pop it into the fridge for 30 minutes to solidify a little, so that it's nice and workable for your little one's hands. I'd suggest that during this time you set up a space for messy mixing with your kids, or take the next stage outside.

Once out of the fridge you can give the bowl to your little one and get into this nutty, oily sensory experience with them. Fill the cupcake tray with the mix. You can tidy up the edges and pat them down as they go (if your inner neat-freak is at its limits!), but allow them to get it all over their hands, making balls with this stuff and overfilling the tray (under filling is more of an issue, as I learned when a couple of our first attempts couldn't pack the punch of being hung up, due to us being far too sparing at this stage!).

When the tray is filled, put it into the freezer for a minimum of 12 hours, although this could also be a return activity a week later should you find yourself bored with bird feeders by this point. Once in the freezer these will last a long time, a feel-good stock of wildlife care and kindness at your disposal.

We took ours out the next day, desperate to see the results, and I poked holes into all the little coconut discs with a pencil. Depending on your child's ability to thread twine through holes, this can then be a joint effort or you can whizz through this part, knotting them all, so now each has a perfect hair-tie-size hanging loop.

Finally, head out into the wilds, the garden or park and put your coconut delights on every eager branch you can find. A bonus if you can then see them from your window, as the flock of visitors will delight your children on a daily basis – for at least three weeks, which is how long ours lasted.

PS The reason these are called cold-weather feeders, is that the coconut oil will melt in the heat . . . these are perfect for frosty days.

Nature hunt

WHAT YOU WILL NEED

Card/paper – cut into postcard-size pieces

Pen, coloured pencils, paints, crayons

Rucksack, magnifying glass

Binoculars, nature fact-finding book such as a wildflower or bird spotting guide (optional)

ENGAGED FOR

At least one hour outside and continued exploring on further walks and outdoor adventures.

PARENTAL ENJOYMENT

I loved making these nature-hunting cards and I always feel good about getting us outside come rain or shine.

GOOD STUFF

Adventure

Body work

Care for animals

Confidence

Listening

Nature

Speaking

Thinking

POTENTIAL FOR MESS

This is a zero-mess activity.

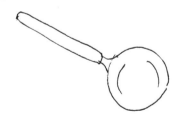

METHOD

Going outside has never been a problem with our daughter Mabel, who loves to jump in puddles, stand in the rain, be barefoot and dig with her hands. However, after a sick bug, which meant a few days of rest, she needed a little more encouragement than usual. She'd got used to the comfort of her 'sick bed' – cosy blankets, PJs all day long and more TV than usual!

On one of the days when she was napping, I decided to make some nature-hunting cards, exercising my own passion for drawing and hoping to create a fun little game for us on our next adventure. I had plain index cards to hand, but you can use A4 paper cut in quarters (the perfect size for small hands), then on each card I drew a picture of something that I knew we could find outside relatively

easily. I chose to draw a simple image of the following; blossom, a leaf, a feather, a woodlouse, a ladybird, a daffodil and, for the final card, dog poo (which made my husband laugh). As long as you are choosing accessible things that you are likely to see (we have two dogs!), then go wild, because the more interesting they are, the more fun you are going to have.

I must have had a lot of time on my hands at that point, because I was very much into this activity so I used watercolours to give the cards life, as well as writing the name of each thing above the picture (you can choose to do this or not, based on your age group).

I put the nature cards into Mabel's rucksack, along with a magnifying glass, then we put on our coats and wellies and out we went, nature hunting!

She absolutely loved having things to find, and to be able to find them successfully, without my help, meant a wonderful sense of achievement for her and it put a spring in her step as she excitedly ran from feather to stick. We used the magnifying glass to hunt out the woodlouse and this became a very thorough part of the hunt as we peeked under pots and logs along our path.

I will make it clear, the dog poo card came with the strong warning of 'do not touch'; however, I was very grateful for the gift of a daffodil.

Nature mobile

WHAT YOU WILL NEED

Long sturdy stick

Natural loose parts

Air dry clay

Rolling pin

Baking parchment

Cookie cutter

Pencil

String

Scissors

Watercolour paints, PVA or Homemade Glaze, see page 61 (optional)

POTENTIAL FOR MESS

This is a mess-free activity because even the clay, which is the messiest component, should be rolled out and decorated on baking parchment to ensure your surfaces stay clean and your discs are easy to move around. (I tried using chopping boards and wooden table tops but the clay stuck to everything except the baking parchment!)

ENGAGED FOR

45 minutes to 1 hour – plus the time spent later, returning to it once your clay has dried.

PARENTAL ENJOYMENT

A mindful, clay meditation with a keepsake at the end of the activity that wouldn't be out of place on Etsy. A sure winner.

GOOD STUFF

Bonding

Creativity

Imagination

Listening

Nature

METHOD

Mabel and I start this activity outside by looking for a sturdy stick and other loose parts that we might like to hang or use to decorate our clay discs. The stick should be relatively straight and strong enough to hold three or four clay ornaments as well as any other nature finds you'd like to include to give your nature mobile life.

Cut off small amounts of clay, so each are about golf-ball size, then roll them in your hands until they are smooth. To get a perfect disc, use a rolling pin to roll it out on a sheet of baking parchment, exactly as you would with cookie dough, then use your cookie cutter to shape it. You and your kids can share out the discs and decorate these however you like. Some ideas might be to press flowers or leaves, feathers or other natural loose parts into the clay to make a print – it's easy for the children to press-stamp into the clay and they'll love to be granted the freedom to do their own. If any of the petals or leaf bits come off into the clay you can pick these out carefully before they dry, or leave them in for a more rustic look. If you want to put the actual flowers or other bits onto the decorations, I'd suggest you dry

out the clay first then stick the flowers down when you are glazing in PVA.

Once you have your decorated discs, get a pencil and poke a hole into the clay, not too near the edge; it may need to be pushed through the other side too once you lift up the disc. The aim is to get some string through when you are ready to hang the ornaments. If you want to let these air dry, leave them for 24–72 hours; however, for a more immediate activity, we pop them onto a baking tray and put them into a cold oven, before turning it up to 150°C/130°C Fan/300°F to warm gently. Check on them in 20 minutes!

Meanwhile, cut a length of string double the length of the stick, then tie it onto each end with a double knot; this will be your hanging string. Now cut 4 (or however many things you have to hang) pieces of string at different lengths and knot them along the stick.

Once the ornaments are dry, you can all paint your pieces (watercolour paint makes for a very beautiful effect on white clay); you can also glaze them or leave them as they are. I must confess, this started as a wind-chime activity but ended up being much better as a visually stimulating ornament of curiosities, so we re-branded this a nature mobile, as we started to tie our discovered items and clay discs onto the pieces of string along the stick. If anyone is going to be a good 'creative director' of a nature mobile, it's going to be your child, after all, it wasn't long ago they were probably staring up at you from their cot – embrace their knowledge!

Mud painting

WHAT YOU WILL NEED

1 cup water

Handful of soil

Small bowl

Paintbrush or nature brush (see p 116)

ENGAGED FOR

10 minutes

POTENTIAL FOR MESS

A lot of potential! This is a messy activity. It should be done at the source, meaning outdoors and if you want my recommendation for how to handle the aftermath, get a bucket of warm soapy water at the ready; you will thank me for that if the mud ends up on your face.

PARENTAL ENJOYMENT

I don't mind mud and getting my face painted – and they do say mud masks are good for the skin? So try to embrace its natural element as best you can.

GOOD STUFF

Adventure

Confidence

Creativity

Imagination

Nature

Senses

METHOD

The joy of soil whilst getting mucky and creative at the same time! In a small bowl put 1 cup of water and a handful of soil and mix together. This can be painted onto pieces of wood, paper, patios (it washes off!!!) as well as, dare I say it, faces and hands! Add more soil for thick mud paint, or more water for a gentle approach.

Nature wands

WHAT YOU WILL NEED

Ribbon/string/wool

Sticks

Natural loose parts

POTENTIAL FOR MESS

Your wand is magically mess free!

ENGAGED FOR

Around 20 minutes, but it makes a great addition to the dressing-up box for a while after.

PARENTAL ENJOYMENT

Nature wands are my go-to, paint free, activity – indoors or out. I love them. The making process quietens busy minds, young and old. As with the other tying activities I encourage adults to step in and do the knotting if necessary, but if you can get your little ones wrapping the string round the sticks then this can go on for a while as the whirling colours dress the sticks and turn them into bright wands right in front of the children's eyes. It is perfect for little gatherings with their friends as it is easy to set up ahead of time, with stick hunting adding a dose of fresh air.

GOOD STUFF

Bonding

Creativity

Listening

Nature

METHOD

'I TURN YOU INTO A . . .' I bellowed at Mabel, as I coaxed her outside into the garden with the promise of a magic wand, clutching my craft materials. This phrase is often brandished around our home, usually turning things into a frog, dog, cat or even a poo – delightful! (The more questionable of spells!)

I put our coloured string and glittery ribbons into a small basket and carried them along as we embarked on phase 1 of nature wand making, which is, unsurprisingly, to find the most wand-like stick! This can go on for a while, because you'd be surprised at how particular a wand is – certainly it can't have any thorny bits, no loose bits of bark and no three-pronged branches coming out of the end. Once you find THE ONE, you will both know it and then it's time to sit down in a quiet spot under a tree or on the grass and let the magic of creativity flow.

We collected some flowers and herbs, too, and much like nature paintbrushes, we bound them to the stick using our coloured thread along the stalk, wrapping it round to secure and then tying a little knot to hold it in place. This was the first time I was taught Mabel to wrap thread, but she got the hang of it after a few attempts and a trial on her finger (which she did far too tightly, prompting me to urgently step in to get her circulation flowing again!). Mabel likes the streamer look for her wand, having received a very beautiful star wand with streams of ribbon from a friend as a present when Peggy was born, which we wanted to replicate, so we tied the ends of three different-coloured glittery ribbons cut to 40–50cm lengths onto the end of our stick like tassels.

Now it's simply time to dream up our big spells and run around followed by a stream of colour, magic and vivid imagination.

TIP

This is great fun for a playdate!

Mix and match pebbles

WHAT YOU WILL NEED

Smooth, flat-faced pebbles

Acrylic paint

Paintbrush

PVA glue or Homemade glaze (see page 61)

Jars or bowls

ENGAGED FOR

20–30 minutes of painting and decorating plus drying time before play commences.

POTENTIAL FOR MESS

Paint can equal MESS, there are no two ways about it. Manage it with small amounts of paint distributed into jars or bowls beforehand.

PARENTAL ENJOYMENT

I love painted pebbles in many forms and have even done mindful craft workshops on this theme. It's also always nice to be able to sub out ordinary shop-bought toys for something you can find in the natural world.

GOOD STUFF

Bonding

Confidence

Creativity

Emotion

Imagination

Nature

Speaking

Thinking

METHOD

I will never forget a little family of pebble ladybirds that I painted at school when I was young. I don't know why they have stayed in my mind particularly, but the image of the red-and-black spotted bugs are etched on my mind, right down to the glossy (PVA) glaze that ensured their durability. They even had their own place on a prominent shelf at home, so my mum must have liked them too! I was playing around with pebble painting with Mabel, who was of course covering them all in grey acrylic paint as I set about creating a little activity for her based on her love of mix-and-match body/face sticker books! I had five perfect pebbles and decided to paint both sides of them, with two sets of eyes, four noses and two mouths. After these had dried,

I covered them in PVA glue, to give them the 'ladybird gloss'.

Kept in a little pouch, these make a wonderful on-the-go activity. If you want to customize the game, you could paint on letters to match objects or even put objects into categories. You'll find that once you start painting pebbles, it's very hard to stop!

Eco glitter

WHAT YOU WILL NEED

Colourful dried flowers

Big green leaves

Scissors

Small glass jar or little glass bottles with lids

ENGAGED FOR

15 minutes – a bit of foraging at the beginning and the cutting and putting together can be stretched out, along with label making and bottling.

POTENTIAL FOR MESS

A bit of floral debris but that's all. In fact, that's rather joyful debris to have!

PARENTAL ENJOYMENT

I wish I'd done this when I was younger; maybe I did in some form during my floral-gathering and outdoor potion-making but certainly there was less awareness about being eco-friendly than there is nowadays.

GOOD STUFF

Creativity

Confidence

Imagination

Senses

Nature

METHOD

The sound of my daughter unzipping my make-up bag immediately sets off alarm bells for me. It's usually lipstick or mascara she's after, but on this occasion, as I leapt through the door to the bedroom, I saw in slow motion the lid being taken off a pot of face-GLITTER! Sadly, I didn't reach her in time to prevent the joyful sprinkling of it into the deep shag-pile carpet, or the bright green, sparkly shower of it all over her face and hair, because a toddler with glitter moves fast! The tricky thing is, I LOVE and HATE glitter – it's a pain in the a*se to clean up, and as it is made of tiny bits of plastic it's bad for the environment, too, but my goodness does it look pretty. I so often want to incorporate glitter into craft; however, I can't face the utter destruction that it brings with it.

I realized that part of the joy of glitter for Mabel is the process of sprinkling, so I decided to start making minimal-mess eco-glitter for her. We use it with glue in the same way that we might regular glitter but it is much less stressful and . . . natural!

Choosing the brightest-coloured flowers you can find, pull apart the petals and place them on a baking tray – you want to dry them out for 24 hours so that the glitter keeps better, so perhaps find a warm spot or sunny window to help them along. Then get some big green leaves and cut them into the tiniest squares. Once your petals are dry you can do the same with them, leaving you with a colourful mix of tiny petals and leaves. Put the mix into a small jar with a lid and use it to decorate pictures, add to your play dough, decorate flower crowns or use as biodegradable confetti!

Nature mandalas

WHAT YOU WILL NEED

Scavenged natural items, e.g. petals, flowers, twigs, leaves, rocks and stones

ENGAGED FOR

20–30 minutes of calm

POTENTIAL FOR MESS

There is the potential for mess when the end product gets destroyed (as I describe below, something you must try to make peace with).

PARENTAL ENJOYMENT

Very beautiful, very relaxing and something I have taken to doing myself (without my children!).

GOOD STUFF

Confidence

Creativity

Emotion

Nature

Senses

METHOD

A mandala is an abstract, circular design ('mandala' is Sanskrit for 'circle') that can be simply coloured in on paper or decorated with natural items. Making mandalas is a mindful practice that creates harmony and inspires a bond and feeling of oneness with nature. The process is quiet and

peaceful and can be done anywhere using the natural materials you have around you. The idea is to create a pattern that radiates symmetrically from the centre.

Encourage your child to start with the smallest things. Lay out your first items, don't worry too much about symmetry. Use bigger leaves and twigs as you circle out the edge of your mandala. It can be as big as you like (or have the patience create). This is a beautiful activity to do together, either working on the same mandala or next to each other on your own. It doesn't need to be perfect and the more you do this, the more creative your flow will be.

Traditionally mandalas would be created by monks and, however long it takes to make them, they then destroy them, to represent that nothing is permanent. This bit shouldn't be too hard if you are doing it with a toddler, so after you've completed your mandala and appreciated what nature has offered you, embrace the destruction!

Flower-ice pie

WHAT YOU WILL NEED

Flowers

Water

Freezer-friendly bowl

ENGAGED FOR

Anything involving picking flowers, or foraging can be customized time-wise to suit you. This creation will need to be frozen which can take between 2 and 12 hours, depending on the size of your 'pie', so factor that in and try to manage expectations.

POTENTIAL FOR MESS

Minimal, but certainly once the melting starts you will want this to be happening outside, or at least on a tray.

PARENTAL ENJOYMENT

It is very beautiful to see the flowers glinting through the ice, and honestly, although I never did this as a child, it takes me back, much like mud-pies, to a feeling of joy in its simplicity.

GOOD STUFF

Creativity

Imagination

Nature

Senses

METHOD

This is the perfect activity for hot summer days. I think I'd best describe this as the warm weather 'mud pie'. We love to pick the flowers together, then put them in a bowl of water and pop it into the freezer. After a few hours, we take it outside and tip the bowl upside down, or crack and scrape into it with a spoon – playing with ways to thaw the ice makes this a wonderful sensory activity.

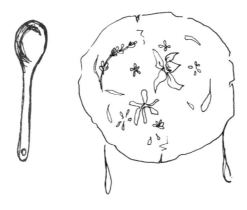

Wildflower seed balls

WHAT YOU WILL NEED

Air dry clay

Soil

Wildflower seeds

Water (optional)

ENGAGED FOR

Making these can take between 15 and 25 minutes; launching them takes a split second.

POTENTIAL FOR MESS

This is a muddy, messy-hands activity and best done outside.

PARENTAL ENJOYMENT

There are whole books on making these for grown-ups, so there is definitely something in it for all of us!

GOOD STUFF

Adventure

Bonding

Confidence

Creativity

Nature

Senses

METHOD

This is a fun project for little gardeners in the making; quick to prepare and perfect for a bit of outdoor soil play that will bring life to a patch of garden or land in a spirited and joyful way. This is a seasonal project, so check on your packets of seeds what month they should be planted in, to give your wildflower seed balls the best chance of getting going.

You will need to pinch off a little air dry clay from your block and make a small cup shape – if your kids need some additional guidance, tell them it's like making a mini tea cup for their teddy bear! In a separate bowl, mix a teaspoon of soil with a few wildflower seeds, then put a pinch of this mix into the clay 'cup'. Pinch it together and all around, sealing in the seeds, then rolling the ball in your hands – if it seems too hard you can add a drop of water onto the ball at this point and continue

rolling. You may be able to see bits of soil through the clay; this is good as it means the mix has dispersed nicely.

In a separate bowl of soil only (no seeds!) roll your clay ball all around until it's well coated. Pop your finished seed balls onto a tray and leave them to dry for 24–72 hours. Once they are dry, you can get to work in the outdoors with your kids – they will particularly enjoy this bit as they seek out sunny patches of soil on which to throw their seed balls. Keep a note of where they landed, then you can make many more excursions outside to watch them grow!

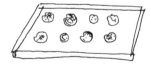

Flower soup

WHAT YOU WILL NEED

Bowls

Flowers

Grass

Leaves

Soil

Jug of water

Saucepan

Spoon

METHOD

We set up our 'mise en place' outside with bowls of cut flowers, grass, leaves and a little sprinkling of soil, all on a tray, ready to get cooking. We added each ingredient in turn to the saucepan of water and made sure to mix them together thoroughly, reserving some flowers and leaves for a garnish at the end. If you want to take this further, why not create a little illustrated recipe card with the things you have picked, then write some instructions or steps for the children to follow, to add another layer to their outdoor kitchen experience.

NOTES, DRAWINGS, INSPIRATION

NOTES, DRAWINGS, INSPIRATION

NOTES, DRAWINGS, INSPIRATION

NOTES, DRAWINGS, INSPIRATION

'Look deep into nature and then
you will understand everything better.'

Albert Einstein

Keep Calm
and Create

It's time to take a long deep breath and with a calm mind and relaxed shoulders, feel assured that this chapter is for the moments when everyone needs a bit of peace and quiet. When things aren't feeling easy, when I want my home to be free from the disturbance of excitable, paint-covered children, or when my daughter wants a bit of independent play within a 'safe zone', I usually turn to the more laid-back activities found on the following pages. In this section of the book you will see that nearly all materials can be adapted to suit a mood, and how the water, arts and crafts, and nature play we've used in earlier can also set a serene and restful scene if you approach each activity with the right intention.

I don't like to use the term 'terrible twos' as it's a generalisation and it doesn't seem fair to label such an important period of time like this, when your child is growing, learning, developing and dealing with so much mental and physical change. However, during the majority of the time I've been writing this book about the therapeutic value of craft, my eldest has been two and I have been continually confronted with the reality of dealing with her newly discovered power. The other day while I was carrying her up some stairs she hit me in the face with a pair of sunglasses and it hurt so much I cried.

Sometimes it's like living with a terrorist. You're not supposed to negotiate with terrorists but you do have to negotiate with two-year-olds. So believe me, I know it's not all lavender and play dough. Sometimes I'd like to call a SWAT team to take over. But I know it's the same for all of us parents and until it becomes reasonable to involve the military police in toddler-related issues, I have included some suggestions for soothing and calming activities that I have found to be very effective.

As with all the activities in this book, it helps if we set the tone with our own approach, and due to this particular theme of hush and harmony, I wanted to share a little nugget I came across recently. It really helped me to shape the way I speak with my children, even when I'm being temporarily blinded by an unlikely weapon. It was an Instagram post that said 'it's possible to change your own brain chemistry by simply whispering', so I took this advice and sometimes when there is a requirement for softness or if temperatures start to rise, I try to stay aware of how I'm speaking, in particular if I'm raising my voice or if I'm being short and irritable. Since using the whispering method, I can hand on heart tell you that bad moods defuse MUCH quicker and I am able to transition into new spaces with my daughter in an easier, less fussy way.

We all know kids have forceful emotions and shouting is often the only way they know how to communicate, but we, as the parent, have the maturity and choice to do things differently. If you whisper to a child in a tantrum, it's likely they will stop – if only to hear what you are saying – and the same applies if you want to guide them into an activity, so why not give it a go, with a whispered 'invitation to play'...

Upcycled shadow puppets

WHAT YOU WILL NEED

Cereal box, cardboard (parcel boxes work well)

Pens/pencils

Scissors

Lollipop sticks/sticks/strips of card/paper straws

Sellotape/glue

Paint (optional)

Torch

POTENTIAL FOR MESS

This is a zero-mess activity, if you leave out the painting . . .

ENGAGED FOR

Around 20–30 minutes to make, then evening after evening of play.

PARENTAL ENJOYMENT

It's a laugh, that has to be said. We made up stories for the characters, too, and even as an adult, once you enter the world of imagination, it is as limitless as a cardboard box.

GOOD STUFF

Bonding

Confidence

Creativity

Emotion

Listening

Speaking

Thinking

METHOD

One dark gloomy morning, when we had nothing at hand in terms of craft supplies, I realized as I poured out the last of the Sultana Bran that with a piece of cardboard, the possibilities were endless. This humble cereal box could be a canvas, a dolls' house, a gift bag or, as was destined on this rainy Saturday, a cast of shadow puppets (inspired by Winnie the Pooh).

Open out the cereal box and draw out your shapes on the plain inside of the cardboard. Small shapes are okay, but the bigger the shape, the easier they are for small hands to decorate and use (and they won't fall apart as easily, either). I made a minuscule ice lolly shape and it was LITERALLY eaten (we were going through an 'oral phase') within seconds. We drew out (using a Google image for reference) the large outlines of Winnie, Piglet and Tigger and I cut them out. We didn't have any lollipop sticks, so I then cut thicker strips of cereal box from the sides and used surgical tape (we didn't have any Sellotape!) to attach them down the backs – enough for a good handle. I then lay them all out and let Mabel decorate them (I gave her the colours to use as appropriate: pale pink and green for Piglet, yellow and red for Winnie . . .), because although decorating is obviously not essential for a shadow puppet, she feels short-changed if a craft activity doesn't include paint. So I happily facilitated.

That night, before bed, we got the trusty iPhone torch on and sat as a family and surprised ourselves with how great our shadow puppets actually were. Oh, except Piglet. Sadly, I had created a horny-eared creature who resembled nothing of Piglet and everything of the Devil. He was quickly banished from the scene to avoid any terrible cereal-box-induced nightmares! However, overall, there was a great sense of accomplishment and fun.

My top tip here would be to create shapes that have a distinctive silhouette. This could be a crescent moon, a star, flower, bunny, butterfly or cloud. There are two templates for you to follow if you'd like a little more inspiration (see page 152-3)

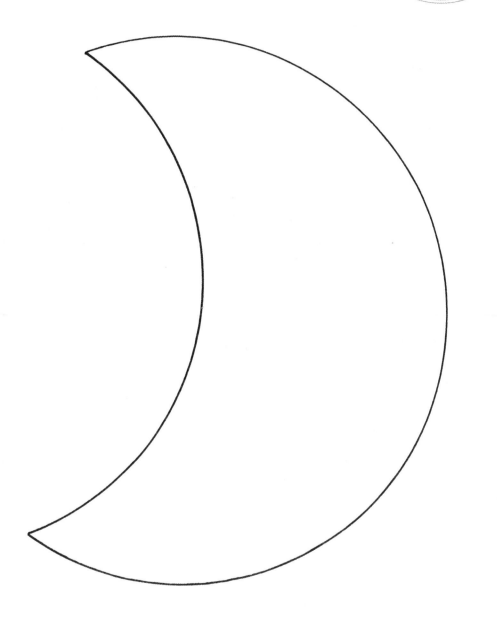

The quiet basket

WHAT YOU WILL NEED

Box/basket/bag/tray

Toys

Pencils/crayons

Paper/stickers

Books

POTENTIAL FOR MESS

The only mess here will be created by using the items and not putting them back. We are still working on 'tidy-up time' in our house, but this is an easy amount of stuff and a good way to start learning to clear up after playing.

ENGAGED FOR

We change the quiet basket every week, and this can take you no time at all or as much time as you want to invest in putting it together. In terms of play, the contents of the basket could create something that your child spends a solid 45 minutes to an hour on, or it could be something that they dip in and out of over the course of a few days.

PARENTAL ENJOYMENT

The enjoyment that comes from this is in the planning ahead. EVERY parent feels like they are winning at life when they set out clothes the night before, have a shower before everyone is awake or, in this case, have a prepped play station at the ready that encourages quiet time and focus.

GOOD STUFF

Creativity

Imagination

Thinking

METHOD

I came across the Quiet Basket idea when I was expecting our second daughter, Peggy. I had read online that it can be helpful to put together a small basket of toys for your older child (18 months old at the time, in our case) so that when you are occupied with the baby, you have something at hand to keep them engaged. To be honest, after the initial horror of seeing me feeding another baby had subsided, Mabel wanted to be involved in helping as much as she could, so  we never found the opportunity to put this into action; however, now she is older, we really see the benefits of preparing a Quiet Basket for the times when everyone needs a bit of calm.

Let me mention ... it didn't start as a success. I put A LOT into the first trial of our Quiet Basket. What I mean by that is A LOT of toys, A LOT of expectation and A LOT of time. I was hoping this would be the perfect diversion from cartoons and when I presented it to Mabel one morning, with over-the-top enthusiasm to see it 'work', she looked at me in horror,

bed-headed and bemused. She then cried and asked for *Peppa Pig*. I was left aghast ... how did I get it so wrong?

Firstly, my enthusiasm that early in the morning was confusing as I am not a morning person, but secondly, I think she probably felt overwhelmed because I was thrusting a basket of toys at her in the hope she'd understand exactly what to do, not realizing that, to her, the basket of toys really represented Mummy not putting the TV on.

To transition this in a way that was more digestible for Mabel, I reduced the number of items to a colourful picture book, a toddler-friendly puzzle, a pencil case with four pencil colours in it and some plain paper, then as she sat to eat breakfast we decided what she would like to do using items from the basket and we did it together.

The success of having a consolidated, small selection of items has led to us now having a theme for our weekly basket. This is much easier for me when I am putting this together, which I do when the girls are in bed, ready for Monday morning.

Here are some themes I have tried, along with a list of items I included:

NATURE BASKET

A scavenger hunt pack

Coloured or patterned paper

Watercolour paints

A torch

A magnifying glass

A nature-based activity book

3 reading books based on nature

MINDFUL BASKET

Colouring book and pencils

3 reading books about yoga, meditation and calm

A mini yoga mat

A wooden Russian doll

A washing-up bowl, with scrubbing brush and tea towel

CRAFT BASKET

Watercolour paints

Selection of 3 paintbrushes

Empty cereal box

Twine

Crayons

Reading book on famous paintings

Tissue paper

Think about things that promote quiet and curious play and *avoid* paints, loud and noisy toys, electronics or complicated games.

The Quiet Basket isn't just for mornings, although I praise it when I'm able to get on top of all the pre-8am tasks without having to listen to any annoying theme tunes, happy in the knowledge that Mabel is occupied with something independently and with curiosity. It is also ideal for when you really want to keep a low-energy vibe or add some 'down time' to your day – you may even like to choose a place for it together, somewhere in your home that your kids find relaxing, for extra cosiness.

Moving and shaking

WHAT YOU WILL NEED

Yourselves

A playlist of good music

POTENTIAL FOR MESS

Zero.

ENGAGED FOR

Between 5 and 15 minutes – customize this to suit you and your kids.

PARENTAL ENJOYMENT

HIGH. This is something that I regularly do with my daughter, and as a family we feel movement really has a positive effect on us. Letting go of our inhibitions in front of our children is good for everyone's mind, body and spirit of play.

GOOD STUFF

Body work

Bonding

Emotion

Imagination

Listening

Self-care

Senses

METHOD

I have included a movement exercise, because I don't think this has ever not worked to shake off stagnant energy, sadness, or ease the mad half hour. The music is optional but I recommend, if you have any time, putting together a family playlist – choose songs with your kids that they enjoy but also ones that you enjoy (because for goodness sake, how much longer can we stand listening to *Baby Shark*!). If you have created this list and have access to it, then it will save you the time and tension of potential Wi-Fi drop out and ensure that you can think about nothing other than getting into the moment.

We start by shaking off an arm at a time, then a leg at a time, then both arms together. 'Shaking off' the body like this releases muscle tension and restores the body and nervous-system. Animals instinctively do this and that's why you might see them shaking off after they've experienced a stressful situation or trauma.

Following our shake off, we take some deep breaths in and out, then we think of how animals move, and start to do a few laps in character. Here are some examples to get you started:

Now let's . . .

Slither like a snake

Hop like a frog

Walk like a bear

Crawl like a crab

Stomp like an elephant

Go slow like a slug

Flutter like a butterfly

Wiggle like a worm

Gallop like a horse

To close off our moving and shaking activity, we stand 'statue still' and bring our attention back to our breathing again, long breaths in and out . . . finding a place of calm, ready to continue with our day.

Coloured rice patterns

WHAT YOU WILL NEED

Rice

Small bowls

Food colouring

Jar with a lid

Kitchen roll

Paper and pen (optional)

ENGAGED FOR

5 minutes of rice prep, then drying out will take 12 hours. Play can be anything between 5 and 15 minutes before their urge to throw the rice in the air kicks in.

POTENTIAL FOR MESS

Start with small bowls of coloured rice; don't give it all at once, this will help mess levels.

PARENTAL ENJOYMENT

It is mindful and satisfying, and much like nature mandalas or a floating flower bowl, ithe concentration will bring a sense of calm.

GOOD STUFF

Creativity

Imagination

Listening

Senses

Thinking

METHOD

I love seeing what everyone does with coloured rice on Instagram (check it out: #colouredrice) – it's incredibly popular for sensory play with toddlers and babies, which is what makes this such a versatile activity. I decided to elaborate on the basic rice-colouring and explore pattern-making using the rice, because, much like the Nature Mandalas, I am interested in art projects as a form of mindfulness, but also activities that can host a calm, quiet environment of focus and beauty. I was worried that my daughter might just see the rice as an opportunity to make maximum mess, and initially I saw her eyes light up as she called it 'confetti'! However, I decided to put it on a tray covered with paper and then, using a pen, draw out simple line patterns for her to fill in with the rice. Giving her the templates helped to bring her focus to a particular place, rather than throwing the rice up in the air randomly. See the following pages for some ideas.

To prepare the rice, put half a cup into a jar, with a few drops of food colouring, then put the lid back on and shake it until all the rice is coated. Now you need to let the colour dry, so spread the rice onto a baking sheet or tray and leave it for a few hours or, ideally, overnight. Once you can touch it and the colour doesn't immediately rub off, it's ready to use.

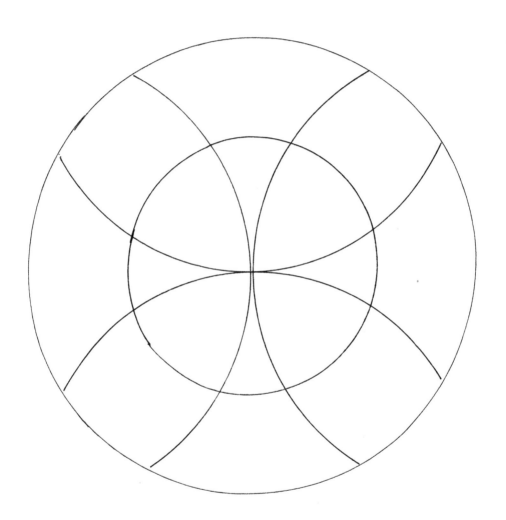

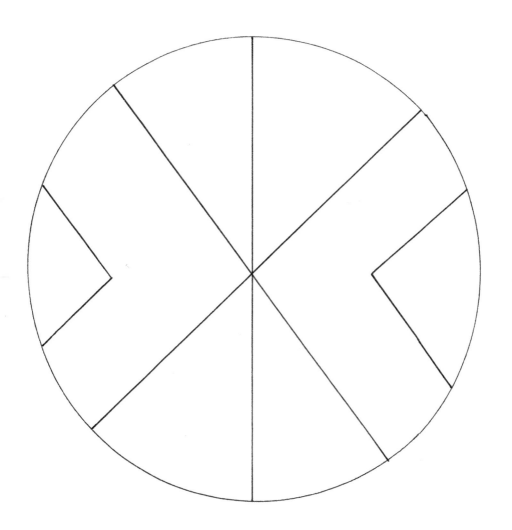

Floating flower bowls

WHAT YOU WILL NEED

Flowers

Petals

Leaves

Bowl of water

Scissors (optional)

ENGAGED FOR

20–30 minutes; add on more time if you are collecting the flowers.

POTENTIAL FOR MESS

There is only potential for water spillage, so to help prevent that danger causing any stress, put your flower bowl on a tray, or better still, do this activity outside.

PARENTAL ENJOYMENT

A very relaxing, peaceful thing to do with your child.

GOOD STUFF

Bonding

Creativity

Emotion

Imagination

Nature

Senses

METHOD

This is as calming and perfect for the grown-ups as it is for your kids, so I really encourage you to try this out for yourself next time you feel the need to decompress. If you have flowers to hand, either from the park, your garden or a bunch of flowers (perhaps looking a little sad and in need of a repurpose), pick off some petals and leaves or flower heads, get a bowl of cold water and sit quietly for a few minutes, creating your own floating flower pattern. I cut the leaves into little strips and chop some of the petals into smaller pieces, then start from the middle with a focal point, working outwards, laying the foliage onto the surface of the water delicately.

If you are keen to follow the same principles of the Nature Mandalas, aim for the pattern to be symmetrical from the centre, but there are no rules here, just the idea that working in this focused way with your hands for a short amount of time (try 5 minutes?) WILL help to reduce your feelings of anxiety and stress and give your mind a calming rest. You kids will love this, too, so perhaps you can all get a bowl and sit together at the dinner table before heading up for bathtime, or maybe it will be just what's needed on a hot summer's day to keep everyone cool, calm and collected.

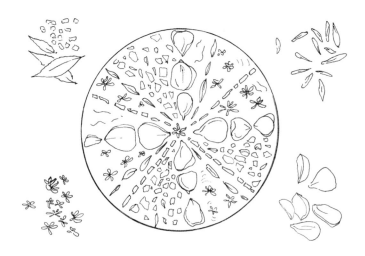

Magic pictures

SHORT
&
SWEET

WHAT YOU WILL NEED

Paper

White crayon

Watercolour paints

Paintbrush

METHOD

If you have ever benefited from those fantastic magic water-colouring books (the zero-mess travel companion of dreams), you could say this is comparable, with the addition of homemade charm.

Write or draw on the paper with the white crayon and invite your little one to paint over the paper with very watery watercolour paints. Watch the miracle in action!

Story bag

WHAT YOU WILL NEED

Paper

Pen

Small bag/piece of cloth and string

ENGAGED FOR

10–15 minutes pre-bed time.

POTENTIAL FOR MESS

Zero.

PARENTAL ENJOYMENT

This can be a wonderfully bonding activity. I understand it's harder when you are managing two (or more) children of different ages at bedtime, so for us this works best when our littlest is already asleep and when we can focus on Mabel's cosy bedtime routine.

GOOD STUFF

Bonding

Creativity

Emotion

Imagination

Speaking

Thinking

METHOD

By the time it hits 7pm I am usually knackered and want to lie down on my bed, fully clothed, and go to sleep immediately . . . HOWEVER, our daughter's bedtime routines can vary in length and time so even a glimpse of a 7pm relaxation time for me is a thing of the bygone era. Thankfully, my husband's unbounded energy carries us through the majority of bathtimes and bedtime stories, but on the nights when it's just me and when none of the usual books are quite cutting it, I have to delve into my imagination and attempt to pull out something magical and captivating (Mabel can be a harsh critic!).

I had the idea, much like a dinner party game, to write words, sentences and names on pieces of paper and put them into a little cloth bag. As part of the wind-down, PJs and bedtime settling routine, we pick out three pieces of paper together and, using these as the three main points to the narrative, we string together our bedtime story. I promise you, minimal delving is required for the tired mind. If you write these when you are feeling like your creativity is flowing, it will make for a MUCH better and more interesting journey into the land of nod.

'Peggy was holding a magic box and it was shimmering bright purple . . .'

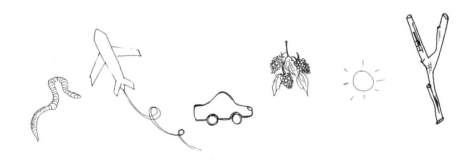

Story Bag Ideas

Personalize the ideas below,
to get started on your journey into story land . . .

Name of
a friend

Favourite Place

A fruit

A type of
transport

Something
from Nature

An animal

An unusual
object

A feeling

A colour

PuRPLE

Peggy

a magic box

Kraft tablecloth

WHAT YOU WILL NEED

Roll of Kraft paper

Pencils/crayons/paints

METHOD

I had never experienced the joy of this as a table covering until we were on holiday and in a restaurant one evening where they had brown paper all over the tables for the kids to draw on using a little pot of crayons. It was a breakthrough; the meal was eaten in full without any fuss. I immediately bought a roll of paper and covered our table at home, and I've never looked back.

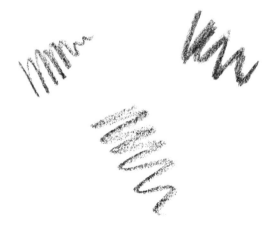

Busy bags

WHAT YOU WILL NEED

Document wallet/
A4 envelopes/bag

Coloured pens, pencils,
crayons

Pencil sharpener

Items that will entertain
your kids and don't take up
too much space

ENGAGED FOR

Anything between
5 minutes and 1 hour,
depending on what you
put into each bag. As
mentioned, you can break
this up for segments of
a journey too, providing
entertainment spread out
over a few hours.

POTENTIAL FOR MESS

I keep mine mess-free by
avoiding mess-prone toys
and craft tools.

PARENTAL ENJOYMENT

This is a very satisfying,
organized approach to
travel and outings when
there needs to be some
calm play.

GOOD STUFF

Confidence

Creativity

Emotion

Imagination

Speaking

Thinking

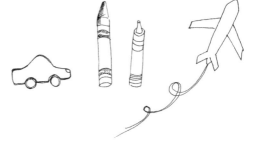

METHOD

I first learned about the busy bag just before a long-haul flight with then 14-month-old Mabel, when I was overwhelmed by the idea of being in a small space with a newly walking baby for 11 hours, so I trawled the internet and asked friends for any tips at all to make it as pain-free as possible (for us and the other passengers). With the advice I acquired, together with an idea I had seen on Pinterest for car-journey play packs, I created a set of four activity packs, split up to cover the amount of hours on the flight. I labelled the packs: 1–3 hours, 4–6, 7–9 and 10–11 hours and only brought out said pack for that specific time frame. The reason for this OCD-style labelling and organizing was that I knew I had the potential to give over everything within five minutes of sitting down, which would ultimately result in boredom striking before take-off. At school, if I was given a packed lunch for a trip or sports match, 99 per cent of the time I'd eaten all of it before I'd even left the car park!

There is so much scope for this, as the idea can be used for car journeys, flights, restaurants or any place with the potential for severe boredom. Once you have the labelled wallets with your activities in, you don't even need to think about them again until you are happily watching your child engaging with toys or sticker books, crayons or small figurines, as the journey time ticks effortlessly past!

I can only advise you from my personal experience by running you through a quick checklist I do to prepare in the best way possible way.

☑ Choose slim, light document wallets, envelopes or bags (like canvas totes), to ensure that the Busy Bags don't become an antagonistic element to your trip.

☑ Don't go for noisy toys – this is particularly important if you are taking these on a flight or using them in a restaurant. If you are including toys for your kids that they already own, try wrapping them up in tissue paper or newspaper, because the element of surprise will be fun addition for them and it also takes up some time when unwrapping them! (Thank you to my friend Annabelle for this one . . .)

☑ If you feel creatively stuck, perhaps use a theme for your Busy Bag, e.g. 'Woodland' – you can put in small figurines of a hedgehog, fox, woodland stickers, flash cards or books about trees, and paper with crayons in greens and browns.

☑ 'Washi tape' is a wonder of a thing. Like masking tape, it can be stuck down on a floor or table to create train tracks, roads for small toy cars or even letters or numbers. It is easy to carry, versatile and easily removed with no damage!

☑ Finger puppets are always a hit with us; another idea to get the creativity flowing would be to choose finger puppets to go with books, to help make stories come to life.

☑ Restrict colouring tools to pencils (don't forget a sharpener) and crayons.

☑ Finally, don't overfill your bags! If the journey is long, work out for how many hours you will need to entertain your kids and divide the time up. Once you've worked through one bag, put it away before moving on to the next one.

Mindful walks

There is no tool list for this activity because all you need is a space to move in and yourselves. I say walk, but this doesn't even mean there needs to be a destination. As a family, we try to practise mindfulness in everyday life. I don't always find this easy and I do need reminders, so please don't think I'm saying this from a position of complete enlightenment! I do try to prompt myself, though, when I find that I'm hurrying my daughter along from some sweet distraction, stealing her joy to rush her to a place of no importance.

When we are walking we generally try to keep very present about where we are; things that can help you with this are to point out trees, the colours of leaves or different buildings, or ask what does the sky look like today – is it cloudy or blue, can you hear a bird or a train, or is there a pretty wildflower growing through a crack in the pavement? Keep the dialogue between you and your kids going, as you walk around freely, or you can even do this en route to school or the shops.

The other day, I found my tone escalating as I shouted 'Mabel! MaBEL! MABEL!' as she smelled a rose on the side of the street. I was pushing Peggy in her pram, it was hot, I had a bag of heavy shopping and we had a long walk home ahead of us. I was irritated that she wasn't listening, I had anxiety about cars passing by too fast, I was calculating in my head that if we stopped at everything we passed we'd not be home for hours and I had work to do – my anxiety was stopping me from being present and I did not handle this as I'd have liked to. I needed to check in, breathe and remind myself of the incredible beauty in her stopping to smell a rose – I mean, it's LITERALLY a phrase! If I could go back to that walk and make a change that I could remember for such future situations, it would be to stop, put down the shopping and join her in that moment and in her joy.

To get inspired, start off with this quick checklist before your next mindful walk:

1. Do you have to be at your destination at a certain time, or can you take it slow? Is there any destination at all or can you go with the flow?

2. Are you dressed appropriately for the weather today? So you don't have to rush home if it rains . . .

3. As soon as you leave your front door, the walk has started. What can you observe right away? Is there a gate to open, a stony path to tread or a bird overhead?

4. Has everyone taken some deep breaths in and out, filling their lungs with fresh air?

5. Seek joy along the way. It will crop up in the most unlikely places.

Homemade bubbles and wand

WHAT YOU WILL NEED

1 tbsp clear runny honey/ agave syrup

1 tbsp washing-up liquid

4 tbsp warm water

Glass jar with lid

Pipe cleaner, or re-use a bubble wand you already have

ENGAGED FOR

Making this takes 2 minutes; playing with it, can go on and on... you may even need to repeat the recipe several times because bubbles never fail to occupy children.

POTENTIAL FOR MESS

There is a little potential for mess in the making phase, possible sticky fingers with the agave or honey. Bubbles are never guaranteed to be mess-free either, due to their nature of popping on floors, walls and clothing... but it's worth it.

PARENTAL ENJOYMENT

Easy to make and always a fun, positive diversion from tears and tantrums.

GOOD STUFF

Bonding

Creativity

Emotion

Senses

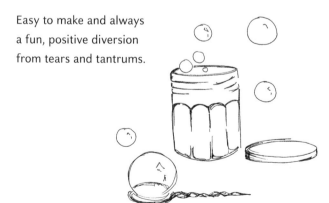

METHOD

Bubbles (a hero activity for most age groups!) are more than just fun, they bring about calm and help defuse tantrums, which means it's always good to have the mixture at hand – 'you can't tantrum if you are breathing and you can't blow bubbles without breathing'. I really wanted to make a 'strong' bubble recipe for the girls, because they love nothing more than blowing and catching bubbles any place, any time, and just sometimes I find we've run out of the good stuff! I could only find recipes that included cornflour or glucose, and when I tried making these they just didn't hold as well as I'd hoped. Once I found out that the thing that keeps the bubble alive is sugar (because it slows down evaporation), I finally landed on this successful recipe using honey.

Mix the honey and washing-up liquid and stir until it's completely combined, then add the warm water and stir again. You will start to see the mixture bubbling a little. If you can, I'd urge you to reuse your old bubble bottles and wands, because if we can limit single-use plastic we are ensuring this activity is eco-friendly too! However, if you don't have any to re-purpose, one pipe cleaner looped at the top in a ring and twisted to hold it is the DIY version. If you are doing this, keep the mixture in a glass jar with a lid between uses (lasts about a week).

For a vegan option, I tested this out with agave syrup and can happily report back that this works just as well as honey in the same quantities as above.

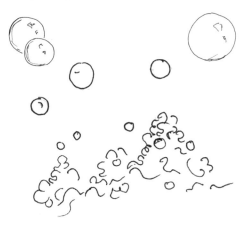

NOTES, DRAWINGS, INSPIRATION

NOTES, DRAWINGS, INSPIRATION

NOTES, DRAWINGS, INSPIRATION

NOTES, DRAWINGS, INSPIRATION

NOTES, DRAWINGS, INSPIRATION

'We need Joy as we need air. We need
Love as we need water. We need each other
as we need the earth we share.'

Maya Angelou

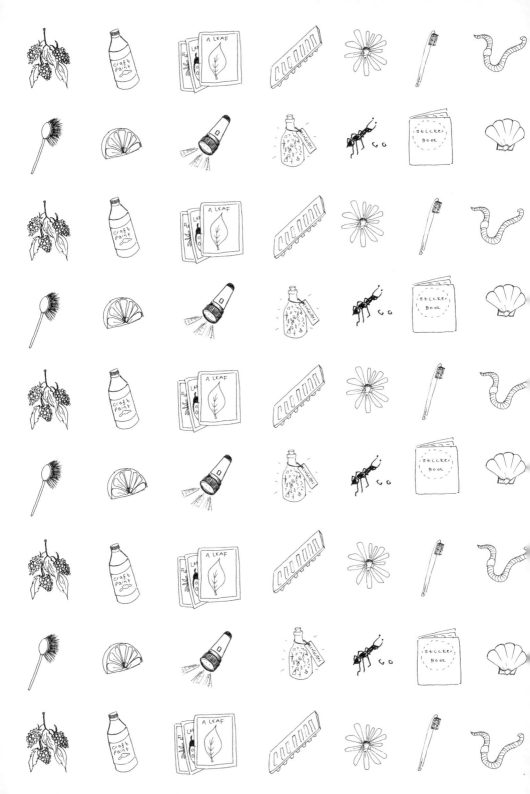

Finding Joy in ...

The playdate

Playdates can be daunting, with mess, mayhem and noise springing to mind, but they are also healthy and fun for your children, good for bonding, creativity, socializing and creating a sense of community.

It doesn't need to be too scary; it is possible that getting a gathering of humans – big and small – around the kitchen table and working on a project together or each on an individual activity, can feel very cosy, there's something traditional about it.

Mabel isn't fully in the flow of regular playdates yet; she generally likes to approach her playdates with an enormous burst of energy, running around in the open air in the playground or garden, then seeming to get overwhelmed quite quickly by the organized group dynamic – certainly we aren't advanced in taking turns with toys yet. I have decided to include a little section on playdates here though, because through my craft workshop experience with two- to five-year-olds (and their parents), I

have learned a few things that make creative play a good option when kids come together.

Rather than 'teaching' everyone to do an activity, I prefer to say it's facilitating a space for everyone to get messy and creative, so here are some guidelines for giving yourself the best chance of preparing a successful arty playdate in the home.

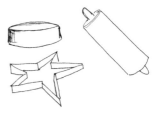

THE KIDS WILL LEAD

Let the kids' energy guide the playdate and don't force anyone to sit and do something, as it will cause tension. With this in mind, let me prepare you by saying the playdate might not end up moving towards arts and crafts, and if so, don't feel your efforts were wasted; keep the materials for your own creative play with your child later that day or the next, or even for another playdate.

PREPARE AHEAD

Do the weights and measures, or gather the twigs and twine, but don't put things out so early that you have to keep telling your child not to touch them (this goes for all art activities); it's much easier to keep it all up high until it's ready to be worked with. The same goes for pouring paint; in case the playdate moves in a different direction, leave this bit until last.

Things to help prepare the space would be Kraft paper to cover the kitchen table, or a washable blanket if you are on the grass. Measure ingredients into small bowls and vessels that the kids can pour themselves. Don't give yourself the bother of waiting on every child when they are all sitting looking up at you waiting for you to get to them, their patience running low. Put materials into the centre of the group, so that they can take turns with them and share them out – this could include tools or loose parts.

KEEP IT RELAXED

This isn't a competition, nor is it incentive-based art – there is no winner. Praise for all should be abundant and encouragement regular. Assist if you think it will help the child, but not in order to control a specific outcome. Children are naturally inclined to be in the moment, so if you are joining in, don't stand in the way of that; practise your own mantra of being 'present in the process'.

OTHER PARENTS

If they are staying with you, invite them to sit at the table and join in with their own project; if the kids are small this is a great way of having another pair of eyes and this offer may bring the parent unexpected joy as well as the confidence to try something similar at home themselves.

ATMOSPHERE AND EXPECTATION

Set a time frame for the playdate, as this will help eliminate any awkwardness and manages expectation, too, which will take a weight off your shoulders. Offer drinks and snacks to children and parents and create or use a go-to kid-friendly playlist so there is music if and when it's needed. As a family, we like to have music or the radio on gently when people come over to create a welcoming environment, and it means there is less obligation for people to fill awkward silences.

Where there is an opportunity to do this outside, take it, but otherwise the kitchen table is fine.

WORKING WITH THE ACTIVITIES IN THIS BOOK

All the recipes in the book are written out for one child so that there is minimal waste. You will need to multiply these based on however many children are coming over.

Here is an example of what a play dough playdate might look like, set out for each child:

JOYFUL ACTIVITIES FOR PLAYDATES

Moon sand (see page 48)

Play dough (see page 45)

Squishy soap (see page 77)

Twig and twine worry dolls (see page 111)

Nature crowns (see page 108)

Nature wands (see page 128)

Nature paintbrushes (see page 116)

Mix and match pebbles (see page 130)

Homemade paints with Kraft tablecloth (see pages 56, 57, 170)

PARALLEL PLAY (WITH YOUNGER SIBLINGS)

Parallel play is when you have children working alongside one another, in an independent way. Interested in, but not directly interfering with, each other.

At present Mabel is nearly three years old and Peggy is sixteen months, so a lot of activities in this book have been written with one child at my feet and the other in my arms. At times I have felt tired, joyful, frustrated, overwhelmed, confused and in too deep, so I hear you when you ask how on earth can you juggle different age groups and create a calm, joyful environment with play and creativity . . .

It's the most wonderful feeling to see children playing contentedly, by that alone, with a friend or, in this case, in a shared space but at their own pace and in their own flow. When you have younger babies, playing alongside their older siblings like this, it can be an important learning experience for them, as they observe the way that their brother or sister engages with an activity, and perhaps even mimics them.

A very successful example of parallel play for my girls, is when I give them both small tea cups and saucers, spoons, little jugs of water and two cut-up cloths set out at their play table. Rather than them playing 'tea parties' they tend to pour their own water, wipe the table or stir with the spoon almost as if the other one isn't even there. Building blocks are another fantastic opportunity for parallel play. I find it particularly nice to start the day by giving them their own small box of bricks to sit with while the sun rises and whilst you grab yourself that crucial first coffee of the day!

When I want to encourage parallel play because a shared activity may be too much to ask of them, I always try to give them almost exactly the same set of tools to use (age dependent); this will limit the chances of them fighting over anything. I also try to give them toys that lead to open-ended play because they provide scope and space for their wonderful imaginations to take over.

I have listed below a few other activities from the book which work for parallel play, so that next time your kids are looking like they want to start some sort of loud, hair-pulling trouble, they can be positively directed towards something much more enjoyable.

JOYFUL ACTIVITIES FOR PARALLEL PLAY

Sensory water play (see page 94)

Kitchen rock band (see page 51)

Magic water (see page 90)

Bubble bath for toys (see page 88)

The quiet basket (see page 154)

Play dough – pre-made and set up on a tray, with their own cutters (see page 45)

Kraft tablecloth – in their chairs, with their own pot of crayons (see page 170)

And WHEN IT'S BETTER TOGETHER...

As well as encouraging parallel play, I think it's also worth making a few suggestions that get the family together and that really work to get young babies and older kids in harmony with each other, because it can be tricky having a few different personalities to manage under one roof, of varying ages. If it's up to me in our household I will always shake off stagnant energy by turning the music up loud and moving around the kitchen, with baby, toddler and husband in tow. So with that in mind, I would suggest:

Moving and shaking (see page 158)

Mindful walks (see page 174)

Upcycled shadow puppets (see page 150)

Homemade bubbles and wand (see page 176)

Resources

PAGE TURNERS

The Montessori Toddler by Simone Davies (2019)

Balanced and Barefoot by Angela J. Hanscom (2016)

The Artist's Way for Parents by Julia Cameron and Emma Lively (2013)

Mindful Crafting by Sarah Samuel (2018)

Shinrin-Yoku by Professor Yoshifumi Miyazaki (2018)

For me-time, tea breaks, recipes and cosy musings, I reach for *The Simple Things* magazine, www.thesimplethings.com

GOOD VIEWING

Ted Talks are educational videos, full of fascinating information presented by experts. They are often short which makes them easy viewing for busy parents. Ted Talks are accessible online (www.tedtalks.com) and on YouTube, as well as on the podcast channel Ted Talks Daily and the TED App. Here are some of my favourites:

Flow, the secret to happiness by Mihaly Csikszentmihalyi

Four lessons in creativity by Julie Burstein

Tales of Creativity and Play by Tim Brown

FOR THE EARS

Podcasts keep me entertained on solo car or train journeys, as well as during dog walks and all the other times I transition from A to B child-free. These are a few of my top picks for channels and episodes:

'Happy Place' by Fearne Cotton: with Elizabeth Gilbert

'Happy Place' by Fearne Cotton: with Philippa Perry

'Respectful Parenting' by Janet Landsbury, Unruffled

'The Slow Home' podcast by Brook McAlary (slowyourhome.com)

'Thriving Children' podcast by Clare Crew: episode 122 – 'Supporting outdoor play' with Angela Hanscom

MATERIALS

Dried flowers and herbs in bulk (although I do love picking and drying them myself): www.Buywholefoodsonline.co.uk

Baby friendly soap bars and liquid soap: Dr Bronner's 18-in-one baby mild pure castile soap: www.drbronner.co.uk

Powdered vegetables and fruit for adding colour: www.justingredients.co.uk

Kraft brown paper and various art supplies: www.hobbycraft.co.uk

Art supplies at good prices: www.art-alternatives.com

The joy of enamelware really comes into its own when working alongside children as it is unbreakable! I use enamel butcher's trays for sensory water play, paint palettes, moon sand and more; you can sometimes find enamelware in vintage bric-a-brac shops, as well as in some kitchen stores. I get the butcher's trays on this fantastic art supply site: www.jacksonsart.com

For mixing bowls and kid-friendly pots for measuring out ingredients, I always try to go for stainless steel as it works well indoors and outdoors, doesn't break and is easy to wash! I like the 'Chef Aid' range, found on Amazon and other online kitchen shops.

Buying a water play table was a really great investment and I always recommend this one to people without fail: easy to put together, a good height for standing babies as well as toddlers, and versatile, it's the 'Flisat Table' by Ikea. Trays and stools are sold separately: www.ikea.com – you can use the trays for sensory water play, moon sand, flower soup, coloured rice, mud pies and more.

I keep every single jar that is ever used in our household. It is washed a couple of times, dried and good to go. I don't think there is a more useful food container than the trusty Bonne Maman jam jars and they look fantastic too: www.bonnemaman.co.uk

For larger jars, I look for Mason ones, which can be bought in packs or individually at the kitchen store Lakeland www.lakeland.co.uk or on Amazon

ONE MORE THING

I often post new product discoveries on Instagram, as well as linking to other great Instagram pages that I follow, where wonderful people spark creative joy and inspiration for families all over the world.

To keep up to date with this, along with activities and workshops, find me @thejoyjournal

NOTES, DRAWINGS, INSPIRATION

NOTES, DRAWINGS, INSPIRATION

Acknowledgements

To Carole, thank you for giving me the chance to write this book. I never could have imagined such an opportunity and I really have deep gratitude for the belief you have in me.

Russell, Mabel and Peggy, what a family I have. Thank you for everything, for all the joy, every day.

Thank you Mum and Dad, for providing me with a loving, varied and nourishing childhood. For accepting my unusual qualities and for all the times I was given freedom to play in nature dusk 'til dawn, digging ponds and setting up camps. You have always supported my endeavours. You make me feel like I'm doing a great job of whatever I have decided to turn my hand to.

Kirsty and Jamie, I am so lucky that I grew up with a brother and sister like you two. You really showed me love and joy and in my earliest memories, I am smiling and looking up to you both. To Erika, for always being interested, loving and supportive.

Oscar and Jude, before I was a mum, I was an Aunty, and I have always had so much fun in that role in your lives. I am so happy that Mabel and Peggy get to grow up near you both.

Debora and Chloe, I genuinely wouldn't have been able to write this book if it wasn't for both of you. We appreciate you both hugely and feel grateful for the help, the comfort and peace you bring to our family life. Chloe, thank you for helping me try out recipes and watching the mess with no judgement!

To Fearne, thank you for always listening to my ideas over the years and being so supportive of everything I do. For writing the foreword to this book, which could not have been more perfect, and for being an inspiration as a

 mother, wife and friend. You always have time for everyone whilst working day and night and I will never understand how you do it!

'The Scoobies', to Mol, Em, Charlotte, La and Soph. What a friendship, one that's spanned all manner of phases, ages and

experiences. It is a rare thing to find a group of friends like you, who stay this close no matter the geographical distance. Thank you all for listening, looking at my drafts of covers and activities, entertaining my experimental photos and endless snaps of my children. Unfailingly enthusiastic. Scoobmen, you too!

To Babs, thank you for being so supportive and interested in what I'm doing. You are a wonderful Grandmother and bring joy, imagination and calm to our home.

Annabelle and Indie, you are both such inspirations to me. Both of you parent to an exceptional level whilst being creative and innovative in all that you do. Thank you for listening to me always and replying day and night to whatever small matter I feel needs your urgent input.

Sarah, Johnnie, Tils, Arch (and Semmalina Starbags), thank you for all the caring and listening at No. 49 and for all the creative freedom you have given me on the shop windows over the years.

For my Godmother, Mary, always a warm home and loving heart, cosiness from every angle.

Nanette, thank you for the Den and the many happy memories I have, growing up.

Sandipan, Anu and all at the Bhaktivedanta Manor. The admiration I have for your endless kindness, service and joy is too great to put into words here. You bring so much to our lives.

Charlotte, thank you for all the flowers, tea, chats and homemade cakes, and for supporting me at workshops over the summer. You made festivals and mess totally manageable!

Amy, you are a great source of my personal joy and a life inspiration – what a relief we were both on that beach at the same time seventeen years ago.

Nicola, you are basically our family, thank you for all the love and nurturing. For supporting me in the early days of motherhood, for being the person to hold our hands on our first trip out with Mabel.

Serena, I am very lucky to have you as my neighbour and my friend.

Lucy, I am positive your crystals have enhanced our lives. Your kindness and spirit is truly beautiful.

Hollie, thank you for being such a wonderful mentor, for teaching me calmness and for helping me so much on the path from pregnancy to motherhood.

Miss Jenny, I really admire everything about 'Montessori', and with this methodology, you have created something very special.

Jay and Kestrel, for being wonderful teachers and showing us how to truly appreciate nature.

Thank you Manya, for keeping me on track.

Charlie and Jen, thank you for being such lovely travel companions and for helping us feel at home wherever we are.

To Cathryn, thank you for being encouraging from our very first conversation and for bringing me into the Curtis Brown family. I am excited for the future. Angharad, thank you for introducing us.

Hockley, Mel, Jess and Jodie – thank you for making me feel so welcome at Bluebird. What a wonderful place to be starting this journey.

Across the pond...

Thank you Miss Faith, for allowing me the space to do workshops on your time and for continuing to encourage my Journey.

To Jeane, for all the love over the years.

Thank you to the residents and volunteers at Union Rescue Mission in Los Angeles, for the play-dough-making joy.

Jeff and Schyler, thank you for sharing your joy with us as a family; we think you are so great and look forward to many years of rock painting in Topanga.

Victoria and Ryron – that boat trip, the lessons we can learn. We really appreciate your friendship and guidance.

Cherise, I'm not sure if there is a person with a greater sense of adventure and joy for the unknown than you. Thank you for being a wonderful inspiration and for always showing those around you how to think outside the box.

And finally . . .

To all the other grown-ups trying their best every day, despite their tiredness.

Thank you to the Instagram community who inspire me and put it all out there for us to see.

Thank YOU for buying this book; I really hope that within these pages I have passed on some of the joy that I discovered when putting it together.

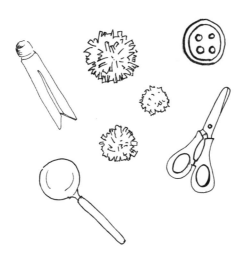

About the Author

Laura Brand is an illustrator and mum of two. She shares her crafty experiments and creative ideas for everyday play on her platform The Joy Journal, and has led workshops for children and adults at Fearne Cotton's Happy Place Festival, Port Eliot festival and others.

Laura lives in the countryside with her husband, their two daughters, two dogs, two cats and chickens. Home is a place of muddy boots, abundant jars of play dough and hand-painted 'welcome' banners above the doors. With chaos and calm in equal measure, Laura aspires to guide her children in the joy of play as well as mindfulness.

Laura has found that having her own creative outlet, as well as facilitating a space for the creativity of her girls, has been a welcome tonic.

NOTES, DRAWINGS, INSPIRATION

NOTES, DRAWINGS, INSPIRATION

NOTES, DRAWINGS, INSPIRATION

NOTES, DRAWINGS, INSPIRATION

NOTES, DRAWINGS, INSPIRATION

NOTES, DRAWINGS, INSPIRATION

NOTES, DRAWINGS, INSPIRATION

NOTES, DRAWINGS, INSPIRATION